The Tropics Are Calling . . . and It's for You!

Lydia A. Estes

and

Robert Kyle Ashton III

Library of Congress Cataloging-in-Publication Data is on file at the Library of Congress, Washington, DC.

ISBN 978-0-5781-1099-8

To view the photos in this book in full color visit:

http://www.tropicsarecalling.com

The Tropics Are Calling . . . and It's for You!

DEDICATION

We dedicate this book to the people with pioneering spirits who are not afraid to risk everything and trek into the wilderness in search of a more fulfilling and meaningful life. It is also dedicated to those who understand that our thoughts are concrete building blocks that allow us to create the ideal world of our dreams.

May the Great Spirit guide you on your path.

To view the photos from this book in beautiful color, go to:

http://www.tropicsarecalling.com

PREFACE

This book is a chronicle of our family's first year living on the island of Ambergris Caye, off the coast of Belize, Central America. Shortly after moving here from the United States we began to make notes in a journal about our experience. These small droplets became a river of descriptions as we secured our new homes, established new careers, and settled into island life. We met hundreds of visitors to the island who wanted to know why we moved here and how we did it. We decided that we would share the answers to their questions in this book that was tentatively titled :"How to move to Belize."

In no way is it intended to be the eighth Ernest Hemmingway novel, or a follow-up to James Michener's "The Caribbean." It is simply our personal story about living on a beautiful tropical island and how that has changed us for the better in ways that we could not have anticipated.

In a nutshell, we learned how to live here by living here. This volume contains pertinent and useful information based on our own experience that will assist those who choose Ambergris Caye as a vacation destination or may eventually want to move to Belize.

Hopefully, you will get a kick out of reading our story and it will transport you to a tropical paradise in the process. May it be a reminder of Ralph Waldo Emerson's astute observation that ... "Life is a journey, not a destination."

TABLE OF CONTENTS

The Tropics Are Calling . . . and It's for You!

Chapter 1

HOW IT ALL BEGAN

My husband Robert has been playing the guitar since he was thirteen years old. After forty-seven years of diligent practice, there are moments when his guitar seems to play itself! When people enjoy his music and refer to him as an accomplished musician, he corrects them by putting things into perspective with his response,. "Beethoven, Bach, Mozart, and Brahms are musicians. I'm just a picker."

One of Robert's strongest musical influences was a singer and songwriter named Jerry Jeff Walker. If you're not familiar with the name, he is the artist who wrote "Mr. Bojangles," his best known and most popular song to date. Countless recording artists have covered this hit song about a talented soft-shoe dancer who Mr. Walker met in a New Orleans lock-up back in 1965. The Nitty Gritty Dirt Band released the song in 1971, and it rose to # 9 on the Billboard charts. The song continues in its' popularity and is a standard on folk-rock stages almost 48 years later!

For several decades Robert and his band-mates have been playing Jerry Jeff's songs in live performance, and more recently in our living room. That is how I became a fan of the "cow-jazz" genre' of music created by this New Yorker who found his true home in Austin, Texas over forty years ago. After listening to, and enjoying Jerry Jeff's songs for many years, I began learning how to play them on my guitar.

On Christmas Eve of '07 we were having a "pickin'-party" in the great-room of our Victorian home. Following our interpretation of timeless holiday classics, we spent the evening playing the rowdy, bawdy, fun songs that Jerry Jeff performed at his concerts over the years. Some of the most accomplished musicians in southern Wisconsin joined us for this holiday hootenanny. It was a special night, filled with easy laughter, extravagant snacks, and superb wine.

Later that evening, after our Christmas guests had departed, we began the task of cleaning up a fifteen room house after the huge party. As we neared the finish line, I asked Robert "Whatever happened to Jerry Jeff Walker? Is he still around? From the stories you've told me, it sounds like he enjoyed more of the fun times and the good wines than most people do! If he survived it all, he should be in his late sixties by now." "I don't really know," said Robert. "We'll have to look him up on the internet." And so we did.

We headed straight for our computer desk. The first Jerry Jeff Walker website that popped-up was titled "Camp Belize." Much to our surprise it informed us that not only was he alive and well, but he was having a concert in a month at a bar called Wet Willy's Cantina. This event was being held on a dock on a tiny island in northern Belize, where Central America borders Mexico.

The website described a week-long affair, complete with a Sunday meet 'n' greet, two concerts under the stars, and ending on Saturday with a photo session and autograph signing with our favorite cowboy singer. It had been years since we enjoyed a real vacation, and the idea of going to a Caribbean island to see Jerry Jeff perform on stage was almost irresistible, and deserved some serious consideration!

We searched a little more on the Camp Belize website and found that there were only two tickets left for "Week One," which was scheduled for the last week of January. "Week Two" was already sold-out, and had been for six months. It was time to make a decision. With the push of a button, the last two seats were reserved for us! Finding our airline and flight itinerary was easy. In just a few weeks we would be on a dock in Belize enjoying fantastic music, tons of sunshine, and warm tropical breezes. We looked forward to this welcome change from the harsh, bleak Wisconsin winter weather that we had learned to tolerate year after year.

A quick digression here: Robert was presented with a gift in 1998. The gift was a CD entitled "Cowboy Boots and Bathing Suits" Jerry Jeff's newest release at that time. It was recorded at the Walker's beautiful vacation home that Jerry Jeff and his wife Susan designed and built right on the seashore of Ambergris Caye, Belize. Robert was very busy at that time, and never listened to it. He gave the CD to "Toto" an old friend and musical- partner to review for him. He was also a Jerry Jeff fan and Robert thought he might enjoy it. Toto gave it a lackluster review. It was not the Jerry Jeff we were all used to. His style had become noticeably Caribbean with hints of calypso and complex Latin rhythms. It was nothing like the old rockin' country music that he was so well-known for. Robert valued Toto's opinion after spending several decades working in the music industry with him. It sat on our shelf for almost ten years collecting dust, un-listened to by us. Off to Belize we went...

"Great souls have wills; feeble ones have only wishes."
Chinese proverb

Chapter 2

DESTINATION: BELIZE

We began our flights with a two and a half hour shuttle-jet from Milwaukee to Houston where we stopped to rest for about an hour. After a snack at the airport we boarded a full sized jet liner which allowed us to reach our final destination in just two more hours. I was lucky enough to have the window seat in the plane. As we were nearing the Belize mainland, I looked out and saw a large shimmering body of water that reflected the most spectacular shades of turquoise and azure and sparkled like a jewel. I had never seen anything with such complex coloring; varying shades of blue, green, aqua, marine, and teal, blending together like a fine work of art. I later found out that it was the Bay of Corozal, the sea that separates Belize from Mexico.

On the horizon, I could see a very definite white line where the 6 to 8 foot Caribbean waves break on the six hundred mile long reef. It seemed to go on in both directions forever. Beginning at the northern tip of the Yucatan, it spans the entire length of Belize to Honduras. It is the world's second largest barrier reef. It protects the beaches from erosion, and provides shallow but bountiful fishing waters along the coast. It creates beautiful color schemes and incredible panoramic views from the sky. It also protects the shoreline of Belize from the crashing waves that come in from the great expanse of the dark blue Caribbean Sea.

The reef in Belize is dotted with many national parks and preserves, and is one of the last living reefs in the world. It is an entire eco-system by itself. It is home to many types of sea life that are very important for a healthy ocean. It is a popular destination for tourists from all over the globe who are attracted to the fabulous diving, snorkeling, numerous water-sports, and trophy-fishing that happens around the island of Ambergris Caye almost every day of the year.

After landing at the Belize International Airport, we basked in the warm sunshine and sultry air before switching to the small 'island-hopper' that would fly us out to Ambergris Caye. This was the island where Jerry Jeff's fans would gather for the concerts. We were very excited at this point and that little plane couldn't fly fast enough. The flight lasted only twelve minutes. It felt like an hour to us!

"I heard" is good; "I saw" is better!

Chinese proverb

Chapter 3

OUR ISLAND DISCOVERY BEGINS

As the tiny plane touched down and the warm moist air filled our lungs, we were overcome with a feeling that "we were home." We had been to tropical countries before, but we were about to discover how this place was different.

When our plane landed, a courtesy taxi was provided by our hotel, Banana Beach. The cab was operated by a helpful and friendly driver named Rocky who took us sight-seeing on the way to our resort. We immediately surmised that no-one here was in a big hurry! We were greeted at our destination by a crew of smiling staff members who were happily going about their duties. Even the women working very hard in the laundry room appeared to enjoy performing their menial tasks. A feeling of contentment was beginning to surround us.

After we settled into our room we headed out to the beach. The water was a pleasant 84 degrees. Warm, yet refreshing. The intense radiation from the tropical sun was very bright but not too hot. The breeze was blowing in gently from the sea, originating from thousands of miles away...pure, clean, fresh air coming all the way from Africa, with no industry or cities in its path to pollute it. Belize is known for its wonderful breezes that keep the island cool much of the year. After hours of swimming in the sea, sunning, and just plain relaxing we rented a golf cart and set out to explore little San Pedro Town. We were hungry for good food and more fun on our latest family adventure.

Our first destination was Wet Willy's bar on the pier where Jerry Jeff would be performing that week. We were trying to imagine how large the dock would have to be to host a concert attended by several hundred fans. It wasn't that big at all. We found a typical boat dock, approximately three hundred and fifty feet long, ending with a 60x90 foot palapa (a pyramid shaped palm-thatched roof) and an outdoor stage. Inside the palapa is Wet Willy's Cantina. It has large open windows on all sides making it easy to view the sea and nearby reef. It was very inviting and we went in to taste an icy-cold Belikin beer while we enjoyed the gentle breezes that constantly pass through the bar.

As we stepped into the shade of the roomy palapa we were greeted by the bar managers, a very pleasant young couple named Kayleen and Garrick. We talked with them awhile and found out that they were from the United States. We were impressed and intrigued that a couple from the States would just pick up and move to Belize.

When we asked the managers about their decision to move here they said "We came here on vacation to go diving and fell in love with Belize. After several return trips we decided to move here. We emptied our house, rented it out, gave our notice to our employers and set out to discover our new life." They went on to explain "You have to have a skill or trade that the government of Belize finds useful to the local community. We are both professionals so we knew that we could find work here. After a couple of years of going through the legalities of attaining a work-permit and becoming residents, we are now welcome members of this little country."

We didn't know that they were asked these questions every day. We had no clue during our first meeting with this adventurous couple, that one day we would follow in their foot-steps. Life is full of surprises!

We were pleased to see that our daughter SierraSky was enjoying the island too. Kids are loved and revered in Belize. Everyone we met acknowledged her when greeting us. She was showered with attention, affection and treats by the locals. Her time on this vacation was filled with joy and awe. SierraSky was even allowed to attend the concert. She had been swimming for hours with her new friends that day, and had played so hard that she slept across our laps, un-aware of the lively party going on all around us.

We enjoyed the concerts at Wet Willy's that week. I would call it well organized chaos. Three hundred and fifty rowdy, fun-lovin' yuppie cowboys and cowgirls having the time of their lives on a dock in Belize! The music performances were easygoing and relaxed. It was Jerry Jeff at his very best. Playing his songs solo and sober, he epitomized the gypsy troubadour songwriter that is now an American icon. The full Caribbean moon was rising above the outdoor stage directly behind him, as he sang "Moon Over My Shoulder" a crowd favorite.

Many of Jerry Jeff's fans play instruments and come to the island year after year for this event. There are numerous impromptu jam sessions and gatherings held on the beaches where some of the best music of the week could be heard. It was inspiring to be a part of all of this home-grown entertainment and the spontaneous cowboy-singing. We never wanted it to end.

There were many things that we enjoyed during our trip; the coconut-palm covered island, the warmth of the people, the beauty and freshness of the sea, the diverse multi-cultural and delicious ethnic foods, the sunshine, the tropical flowers and plants, and the numerous species of birds gliding on warm air currents in the blue sky. We were impressed with the easy smiles and the slower pace of life that the islanders all seemed to share. The lack of traffic, stoplights, police cars, and franchised stores was a welcome relief from our hectic life in the United States.

Aside from the country's stunning beauty, the natives have a kindness that is unsurpassed by any culture we have experienced. We found that the Belizeans have a very mellow, life-is-good attitude. They smile a lot and it seems like they have a pleasant secret. They live and work at such a casual pace; there is no rush in their step, no stress in their gait. We came here thinking that the warm weather and spectacular reef were the main attractions for this tiny island's numerous foreign visitors. We soon discovered it is the residents of San Pedro town, and the unusual mix of 12 distinctly different cultures that make this country unique, and therefore so popular.

The locals made us feel right at home as though we were visiting old friends. It became our personal mission to find out what's in the air in Belize that has such a positive effect on its society. We hoped to breathe enough of it to fill our souls with whatever it was that was making them happy with their simple lives and their everyday routines.

More often than not, it's too soon when the last hours of a vacation finally arrive. The day you leave this tropical paradise on the single engine island-hopper back to Belize International airport is called your "Sad Day." We found out why…and we totally agree. Belize: hard to get to; even harder to leave! Alas, all too quickly, it was time to return to our winter wonderland. Sadly, we faced the facts. The dream was over…for now.

You have probably seen video segments on the news of suspected terrorists being pulled off a plane at some distant airport, kicking and screaming. That is what the scene was like when trying to get Robert BACK ON the plane to the United States. He did NOT want to go back home. He said: "I want to live here forever, starting today." Fortunately, my response was "Me too!" We made a deal on the spot: If he would come back to Wisconsin and help finish the restoration of our home, and help to complete our business projects, we could come back to Ambergris Caye to live one day.

"Man is the head of the family, woman the neck that turns the head."   Chinese proverb

Reluctantly, Robert boarded the plane with us and we headed home to Wisconsin. On the flight home we began to develop a 'five-year plan' that would allow us to move to our newly discovered tropical paradise. As we headed home, we reminisced about our trip. We had been impressed with a very positive experience. Could we really find a happy and meaningful life for our family in the third-world tropics? As we weighed the plus-minus comparisons to our life in Wisconsin, we decided that a move to Belize was definitely possible. We also agreed that we would make a practical and realistic plan to live where people are happier and more relaxed; a place where the children are safe, can walk to school, and can grow up without fear; a place of peace and serenity.

Shortly after our return home, we finally listened to "Cowboy Boots & Bathing Suits" the Jerry Jeff album that had sat on the shelf in our music room for ten years. Our eyes welled up with tears. The songs were written about our trip to Belize. The album captured the feeling of little San Pedro Town, the local people, the places we had been, and just about everything that we had seen, eaten, or enjoyed on our eleven day vacation. Listening to this CD often helped us to keep our dream of moving to Belize alive.

February was cold and dreary as usual in Wisconsin, and it felt like the time was right to announce to friends and family that we were serious about moving to a tropical island. No one really believed us. They giggled nervously as they asked questions about our plan. "Have you lost your minds?" "What about your home? Your business? Your family, and friends? You have a daughter who is ready to enter school. You can't just pick up and move to a third-world country." We didn't listen to the nay-sayers for one moment! Our minds were made up.

"The person who says it cannot be done should not interrupt the person doing it."

Chinese proverb

Chapter 4

PICKING UP AND MOVING

Our friends and family continued to doubt that we were actually leaving and starting new lives in Central America until we booked our flights to Belize. When Robert's mom and sister realized we were serious, they asked "Can we come too?" We said "Sure! The more, the merrier." Twenty-two months after our visit to Belize, Jo- mama, aunt Cindi, Robert, SierraSky and I set out on our journey to paradise. We never considered the possibility of failure. All we knew was that we wanted out; out of the cold, out of the rat race, out of the frustration and difficulty of the Northland. The definition of a true adventure is not knowing what lies ahead. What we did know was that our day to day life in the United States was a lot like watching re-runs on TV. It was time for a change…

There we were, in the Belize airport with our fifteen suitcases, four guitars and a mountain of carry-on items and purses. Our plan was to enjoy our first week in San Pedro town at Mata Rocks, a beautiful resort on the sea. After relaxing for a few days, we would start the search for our new homes and begin to explore the island. With Hurricane Ida looming in the Gulf and very little money in our pockets, we were filled with hopes and dreams.

Our rooms were cramped with all of our personal belongings. Most guests at Mata Rocks are there for vacation, and aren't planning to stay forever. The employees looked at us and our pile of luggage. We could read their thoughts from the smiles on their faces. "Gringos, new on the island, dreaming beautiful dreams, with stars in their eyes!"

SierraSky absolutely loved the pool and we enjoyed the little tiki bar called the Squirrels Nest on the beach. We laughed a lot and made friends with the attendants at the resort, who showed us their genuine Belizean kindness and hospitality.

Our first morning in Belize was picture perfect! It was time to explore the island. Golf carts are the main form of motorized transportation in San Pedro town, second only to bicycles. We rented a cart, squeezed five people into four seats, and headed north to San Pedro town.

It was enjoyable to see the colorful and diverse flora again. Hibiscus trees abound, ficus trees make solid walls, and the graceful palm trees swaying in the breeze are an island trademark. How wonderful to be in paradise again and to share it with Robert's mom and sister. It was fun to watch them discover what we had seen on our previous trip; the hummingbirds hovering over the flowers, the blackbirds making a sound like a slide whistle, the butterfly's fluttering amongst the fresh blooms, along with several types of iguanas and lizards basking in the warm sunshine. Of course it is impossible to miss the turquoise sea and its breathtaking beauty. The water is always a different color of sky blue, emerald, dark blue, light blue, green, and sometimes even purple at sunset. Time passed slowly as we searched for the perfect home on the sea…

"If you hurry through long days, you will hurry through short years"   Chinese proverb

Chapter 5

CHOOSING OUR CARIBBEAN HOMES

For the first couple of days in San Pedro we bounced around in our golf cart looking at possible houses, condos and apartments to rent. You aren't allowed to own a golf-cart until you secure your residency, and after becoming a resident it is still difficult to qualify for the ownership of a cart. We were offered a great deal on a long term lease from Polo's Golf Cart Rentals.

Everyone and their sister seemed to know of a house or an apartment that was available to rent or buy. Most islanders don't spend their precious money on an ad in the local paper. Instead, most landlords use the "coconut telegraph" and rent their apartments by word of mouth. After talking to several local families we were confident that we would find the ideal place for all of us to live. We arrived in Belize just before the high season began. The housing market was still wide open and people were eager to rent.

Most of our first appointments to look at rentals were down south by our hotel. We didn't have a view of the sea from any of them. There is a vast difference between looking out your window at the great sea, and walking a block to see it. We ventured north of town to where the reef is closest to the island and the ground is higher above sea level. The acceptable apartments ranged in price from $500 USD on the lagoon side, to $1500 USD on the beach. There are neighborhoods where tiny dwellings are rented for $200 USD per month.

The lagoon is the body of water that lies between the island and the mainland. There are many smaller islands and sand bars between Ambergris Caye and the mainland. The lagoon is not like a lake or pond, it is part of the ocean but more placid. Living on the lagoon side of the island has its ups and downs. Breath-taking views of the sunset can be seen from that side and the fishing is good in the calm waters. We preferred the beach side and crossed our fingers in hopes that we would find a house that was right for all five of us.

Sometimes I think Robert is a luck magnet! We found a cute little bungalow on the beach with a "for Rent" sign in front of it for $650.00 USD, and there was a larger apartment for rent a few doors down for $800.00. When talking dollar amounts in Belize, everyone uses Belize dollars except when talking about real estate which is priced in USD.

We had a family meeting and discussed whether we were willing to move into two, one bedroom apartments instead of one four-bedroom home. We discovered that there weren't any four-bedroom homes for rent on the beach. The only way we could enjoy the luxury of living on the sea was to rent separate dwellings. The apartments were small but we all agreed it was a sacrifice worth making. We had found our beachfront homes! After all, the sea, the palm trees, the beach, and the waves breaking on the reef were the reasons we moved to Ambergris Caye, Belize.

We quickly located the landlords of the apartments and secured our leases on the last day of our stay at Mata Rocks. Our new landlords were very surprised that we needed to move in immediately. No problem. It is the Belizean way to be very accommodating. They even offered to help us move in that evening.

Robert, SierraSky and I chose the one bedroom apartment at Emerald Reef Suites and the bedroom was so large that it had two king size beds in it. The ceilings were twelve feet high and the floors were cool, white, ceramic tile and easy to sweep the sand off. Jo-Mama and Cindi chose to share a not-so-large bungalow a few doors down, but the breath-taking view from the beach-front lot couldn't be passed up by anyone in their right mind. Everyone's version of God is different, but we knew the Universal Force was working with us that day, and everything fell perfectly into place. We were elated to be in our new homes on a tiny island in Belize!

The Belizeans made us feel very welcome. They were genuinely curious about us and stopped by often to see how we were doing. Many visitors had tried to live here, but eventually returned home to the United States. We felt as though the San Pedranos were rooting for our success as the newest guests on their island.

"If we don't change our direction we're likely to end up where we're headed."   Chinese proverb

Chapter 6

OUR ISLAND DREAM BECOMES REALITY

After a few weeks on Ambergris Caye, the reality of living our tropical dream finally set in, and the feeling of being on an extended vacation slowly began to fade. Each morning I would find myself eager to open our floor-to-ceiling drapes to see the sunny blue sky and the palm trees blowing in the wind. I would re-confirm to myself that we were really living here, and that our vacation was not coming to a close as it had in the past. The feeling of having to go back to the cold, harsh Northland started to slip further and further into an old nightmare from a previous life. Vacationers leave here every day and their long faces are a dead give-away that it is the well-known Sad Day of departure. We hoped that we would never have to leave this place again!

It was such a joy each day to wake up and wonder what unusual creature I would see, like a gibnut, a huge rabbit-like rodent, or a coatamundi. It was also interesting meeting characters that we would encounter on the street. We were having fun discovering the local markets and fruit stands and all the unique San Pedrano stores. There are scores of fruits and vegetables that weren't available in Wisconsin, a bountiful supply of fish and seafood, and plenty of locally raised meats.

Meal time was an adventure three times a day. There are countless exotic new dishes in Belize that we could sample. Foods like papusas, salbutes, garnaches, and endless choices of soups from different ethnicities. We sampled a black pepper soup with pork dumplings and hard boiled eggs called "chili relleno," and the very popular "cow-foot soup!" They were both delightful and pleasing to the palate.

The national dish of Belize is rice and beans with stew chicken or beef and is usually served with sides of coleslaw and potato salad. When we first ordered it we thought we were going to get chicken with a side of beans and rice. We soon came to realize that "rice and beans with stew chicken" meant just what it said. You are served a mountain of rice and beans (way more than I could ever eat in one sitting) accompanied by a tiny side of meat, potato salad and coleslaw. You can also add a delicious spicy habanero-onion relish to sprinkle on top. It is filling and delicious.

One dish that we did not find appetizing was the "chicken ceviche." Unlike the delicious "shrimp ceviche" which is made with fresh lime juice, cilantro, tomatoes, onions, garlic, carrots, cucumbers and habanero peppers, the "chicken ceviche" combines all edible parts of a chicken in a warm grey broth. It includes the feet, back, neck and organs. It smells like cooked liver and is a Belizean delicacy. It must be an acquired taste.

There are countless food vendors on the streets (all licensed and inspected) and $3 USD will buy you a delicious snack or meal. An epicurean's paradise! During lobster season (June 15 thru February 14) the vendors sell a 'lobster-burger' in the park. It consists of a grilled lobster tail with your favorite sauce, on a hamburger bun and costs only $5 USD. We try not to eat too many of them...

Every Saturday the locals serve barbecue chicken on the street corners throughout town. The streets fill with the smoky essence of barbecue sauce, dripping and burning in the flames. Robert and I would look at each other and say "It's Saturday! Can you smell that wonderful barbecue?" We noticed the weeks passing by when it was barbecue chicken day again, just like the old days in Wisconsin, when we would notice another week had flown by with each Friday night fish fry.

In late afternoons, locals come out to the pier docks and watch the fisherman clean their catch of the day. We all watch the pelicans happily swallowing the fish parts left after filleting the fish, while the frigate birds circle overhead on the warm air currents, hoping to be tossed something too. Stingrays swim in the shallows waiting to be hand-fed by the fishermen as small crabs compete for the scraps.

We were saddened to see each day end, but very excited to see the next one begin. I would always try to take a dip in the sea before the sun set. A swim in the cool water is like a relaxing bath after a long day in the sun. It is invigorating and rejuvenating! Belizeans think that it is healing to soak in the sea due to the high mineral content of the water. The beautiful children, whose skin-tones range from light brown to dark coffee, laugh and splash in the water.

When the sun sets and nighttime visits the island again, you can hear the kids playing in the streets. It is common to hear the delightful sounds of their spontaneous laughter well into the evening. In Wisconsin, we would rarely see children playing outside after dark.

The people in the town of San Pedro were helpful to us gringos. They were teaching us how to survive in their very special world and we appreciated all the ways that they helped us adjust to our new way of life.

"The journey of a thousand miles must begin with a single step."
Chinese proverb

Chapter 7

TIME TO THINK ABOUT WORK

All too often in life, reality rears its ugly head and practical choices must be made! Sadly, we had not come to Belize to enjoy an early retirement. Robert, Cindi and I realized that we needed to start earning a living. We began thinking about how to generate income.

Cindi mulled over many plans in her mind, exploring her talents and considering her options. She was leaning towards child-care as her specialty. She decided that she would visit all of the elementary schools and pre-schools and propose after-school care. We heard that the required work permit is hard to get and expensive in this country. But, where there is a will, there is a way.

I thought I would leave my old career behind but there seemed to be a need for pet-care on the island. I had become an expert in pet nutrition and dog-handling, and could offer pet-sitting for ex-patriots that might want to go home to visit family or take a vacation in the States. There was only one kennel in town and it was usually full to capacity! If I was going to get involved with the pet care field again, I knew didn't want to do boarding, grooming, healthy pet-foods, training, pet-sitting and dog walking this time. I considered only pet-sitting as a possible career choice.

Robert could often be found sitting on the front porch playing his guitar into the wee hours of the night. He thought that it might be time for him to go back to live performance after a twenty year hiatus.

At Emerald Reef Suites, a man who was also named Robert lived across the hall. He happened to be a talented guitar player. We were delighted to have him as a neighbor. The "Roberts" would play for hours, entertaining the other members of the condo building, the neighbors across the street, and the occasional tourists walking by. People really enjoyed the live music. We decided that performing music for tourists could help solve our financial dilemma. We knew it wouldn't happen overnight and it would take time to research and find out the legal process of acquiring work permits.

We had a great time discovering the music scene in San Pedro town and getting to know all of the local musicians on the island. Dennis Wolfe and the Usual Suspects was our favorite band, right from the start. Dennis is originally from Florida but moved to the island over twenty-five years ago. He wrote a song entitled "Just Another Gringo in Belize." It's the story of a typical dreamer who comes down to Belize and spends too much money, makes bad investments, drinks too much rum, and goes straight home after losing everything he has! It was written with sympathy and humor, and it is generally accepted as a song about Belize that has a lot of truth in it. Jerry Jeff Walker liked the song so much that he recorded it on his album "Cowboy Boots and Bathing Suits." On his frequent visits here, Jerry Jeff and Dennis sing it together on stage.

Another band was named All Cayed Up (pronounced "keyed"). They are a Chicago-style blues band. We enjoyed listening to some down-home blues!

We discovered Gino's band, Relejate, from Harvard, Illinois. There was also Dale and Walfredo who played Belizean music and steel drums. A younger crowd pleasing duo from Dallas, Brandi and Tull, had a band called Love Paradigm. We were happily surprised to find Russell Hulme, a very tasteful musician with nice arrangements, played at a volume that you can hold a conversation over. He performed a solo act of smooth blues and jazz guitar.

We were pleased to find out that the locals had a real desire to hear some fresh sounds from a new band. They had been listening to the same bands for years and needed some variety. One night while the "Roberts" were playing, I picked up the bass guitar and tried it out for the first time. I was thrilled with it, and the learning process began. I have always loved music and getting paid to play it sounded like a fun way to earn a living. Time would tell...

"Be not afraid of growing slowly, be afraid only of standing still."

Chinese proverb

Chapter 8

BELIZE IS LIKE A PERFECT SUMMER DAY

I don't know about you, but as a child I always LOVED summertime! No school, hot sunny days, swimming at the lake, riding bikes, picking peas and beans out of the summer garden with my mom. I remember romping with friends from early morning until dusk. We played tag and hide-n-go-seek, climbed tall trees, and even made up our own fun 'n' games. We would go to the park to swing and play and then ride our bikes across town and back again. It was mostly good times, and plenty of great memories come back to me when I think about my summers in Wisconsin.

Since we moved to the tropics, it feels like summer every day. That doesn't appeal to everyone, but it's a perfect fit for me. My life here is generally more positive and cheerful, without the ever-present threat of cooler weather always looming in the distance.

Each fall in Lake Geneva the green leaves start turning colors because of colder temperatures, and there is less and less light each day as the sun makes its long journey toward the winter solstice. Soon, the trees are stripped down completely and are prepared for the long, harsh winter that lies ahead. This whole process was so depressing for me. The annual struggle that comes with trying to battle nature and to survive in an icebox for six months doesn't exist in Belize. We don't suffer from a lack of sunlight, endless low cloud ceilings, stalled fronts, and the numerous passing storms caused by low-pressure gradients. Here, we have hundreds of consecutive days of sunshine, broken up by an occasional tropical rainstorm. The sun returns almost immediately after an un-expected fifteen minute cloudburst. This is a place to celebrate the sun, the gorgeous flowers, and the lush green plant-life that surrounds us every month of the year. The "winter blues" are almost non-existent.

There is plenty to be said about blue skies and sunshine. It is a fact that vitamin D from the sun can help to boost ones' spirits and immune system. One of the first things you notice when you arrive here, are the easy smiles that seem to be on everyone's face. "It's gotta' be, the vitamin D!" And we all agree, everyone looks better with a suntan.

My personal preferences are to be sailing among turquoise waves rather than ice skating, fishing at the end of a long boat dock instead of trying to stay warm in a Wisconsin ice-fishing shack, and wearing a sundress instead of a snowsuit or a parka. I prefer rainstorms to blizzards, flowers to icicles, sandcastles to snowmen, swimming and waterskiing to downhill or cross-country skiing, outdoor bar-b-cue cookouts versus gathering around the fireplace to beat the cold.

Wisconsin is warm and sunny a couple months of the year. There is no comparison between where we came from in Wisconsin and San Pedro Town, just 17degrees north of the equator. It is toasty-warm, enchanting and easy on the eyes every day. There is a celebration or holiday every week. Smiling, friendly, happy people are the rule, rather than the exception...and don't forget every Saturday is another 4th of July cook-out. Fabulous foods and cool beverages of every kind, it is a Cancerian beach-bums' dream come true! I am truly in my element, here. I love summer, and I love Belize where every day has a little bit of summer in it.

"Summer afternoon...Summer afternoon... the two most beautiful words in the English language."

Henry James

Chapter 9

THE BEST CHRISTMAS EVER

Wow! Was that Christmas? I really have to pinch myself. It sure didn't seem like Christmas. We were used to snow, gray skies, freeeeeezing weather, slush, cold winds, dead batteries, frozen windshields, salty cars, and shoveling out the driveway! Somehow, I found myself on the beach enjoying the white sugary sands and swimming in the 83 degree sea with SierraSky. She had just received a little pink swimsuit from Santa and was eager to test it out!

We had a picture-perfect Christmas day in San Pedro; sunny blue skies with big white puffy clouds. The sea was calm and the surface was like glass. The shades of blue in the water were such a treat. It's like candy for the eyes and soul. As I sat there, relaxing under a palm tree and making sure there wasn't a big ripe coconut about to fall on my head, I kept telling myself "Yes, it really IS Christmas, Lydia!"

Robert was at the vegetable stand when a fisherman approached him with his catch. He offered Robert the deal of a lifetime on some lobster, but Robert didn't have much money on him. The fisherman said "$70 (Belize) for five pounds". The average price is $25 BZD per pound. Robert said "Well, that's a great price for fresh lobster, but I only have $40 BZD with me." The fisherman said "I need to buy my kids some presents for Christmas, I'll take it." So, Robert procured a five pound, fresh-frozen bag of lobster for $4.00 USD per pound.

Our first Christmas dinner on the island was not the usual turkey, ham, dressing and potatoes. Instead, we had a seafood medley of shrimp, lobster, and more lobster. Robert prepared it perfectly using coconut cream, garlic sauté, and broiled snapper with Caribbean vegetables as side dishes. Our friend Floyd said it was the best Christmas dinner he had ever eaten.

Christmas on the island was very special in many ways that year. Christmas Eve exemplified the true spirit of giving for us. We were included by Dr. Floyd Jackson to be a part of the "Free Christmas in the Park." Dr. Jackson is a gentle beneficent soul who has retired here on the island. He has been in the medical and psychiatric fields for decades. He only practices in emergencies these days. Instead, he teaches the youth how to play music at his "Free School of Music." SierraSky joined his class, and began learning how to play the piano. Jo-Mama was a classical pianist and encouraged her to practice every day.

Dr. Floyd sponsored the Free Christmas event for its seventh year. He collects donations and provides hundreds of gifts for the San

Pedro boys and girls. Some families have' no extra money and cannot afford gifts for their children without the generosity of a patron. He also purchased several turkeys, a delicacy on the island. He asked us if we would like to help him out with the event and we happily joined in the effort.

We cooked a traditional American Christmas/Thanksgiving turkey dinner with mashed potatoes, stuffing and gravy, sweet carrots and cranberry sauce. Another volunteer, a Garifuna woman named Handa, cooked her turkeys Belizean-style with rice and beans. We portioned the meals into almost one hundred total dinners. We happily dispersed the dinners in Central Park, and families shared meals with their children. No one attending the 7th annual holiday event went to bed hungry on that Christmas Eve.

Aunt Cindi was also an important contributor to our Belizean Christmas Eve. After wrapping the hundreds of gifts in newspaper and delivering them all to the park, she was asked to lead the kids through the traditional Christmas carols. Listening to the Belizean children singing Here Comes Santa Claus, Frosty the Snowman and Rudolf the Red Nose Reindeer, was a sight (and sound) to remember as a part of our "Best Christmas Ever."

Robert was at the right place at the right time again and was lucky enough to play Santa! When we heard the island Santa was having some health problems, the natural second choice for the job was Robert. He had practiced the year before when we offered photos for customers and their pets with Santa at The Dog Spot, our business in Wisconsin. It was endearing watching the young kids with their big brown eyes, standing in line patiently waiting for their presents.

"A turkey never voted for an early Christmas"

Irish Proverb

Chapter 10

AN ARCTIC BLAST CHILLS THE CARIBBEAN

We were experiencing record-breaking lows the second week of January in San Pedro Town. On January 11th the temperature dipped to 60.4 degrees with a wind-chill of 48! This was an all-time record for the island. After eight weeks of enjoying temperatures in the upper eighties, our blood must have thinned out because it seemed very cold to us. We were the recipients of the tail end of an Arctic clipper that came all the way down across the United States and into Mexico. It was snowing heavily in the mountains surrounding Mexico City! To date, they have no snow plows or road salt in this part of the world.

My friends in Wisconsin did not have much sympathy for me or my whining about our "cold" temperatures in the upper fifties. Recently, they had suffered through nights that were below zero degrees and shoveled their way out of several huge snowfalls. The Arctic clipper wasn't as kind to the States as it had been to Belize. They had record breaking low temperatures in Arizona, New Mexico, Texas, Louisiana, Georgia, and Florida. The orchards had gone below freezing and the local news was full of warnings of increasing fruit and produce prices.

People were saying sarcastically, "Oh yeah, global warming is here all-right," as they experienced some of the largest snowfalls since weather records have been charted. This is exactly what the global warming experts were warning would happen. As the polar caps warm up and begin to melt, icy cold water flows like rivers into the ocean. This affects the ocean currents and eventually the jet-stream, which then disrupts the global temperatures. The result is that the coldest air on record has been pushed all the way down here, 17* north of the equator. We are shivering in the tropics and I heard it was forty-four degrees in Antarctica the day before.

"Global screw-up" is probably a more accurate term for the greenhouse effect as the jet-stream begins to change its direction from north to south more frequently, instead of its usual pattern from west to east. It was definitely out of the ordinary to see the sun-tanned Belizean dressed in winter coats. The Canadians were getting off airplanes and keeping their coats ON!

Some of the locals say "It gets cold every winter for a few days." Others reported "This is the coldest weather that I can remember." The older, wiser ones tend to be the ones saying these are record-breaking lows. There aren't many thermometers around, certainly no electronic bank signs announcing the temperatures, and we had not found any local weather coverage on TV. We didn't know exactly how cold it was, if it was typical, or if the coldest week in recent memory had made history.

Even the green iguana that lived in the ficus tree outside our front door was hibernating. We looked forward to warmer temps in the coming weeks. The average is 84 degrees year-round. Typically, temperature is 86 degrees during the day and 80-82 degrees after the sun sets. When we moved to the island, we brought a down-blanket along. Who knew we would actually need it someday?

"Winter is on my head, but eternal spring is in my heart."

Victor Hugo

Chapter 11

A CHILD'S PARADISE TOO!

As parents, we were concerned that our daughter SierraSky would miss the United States and all of the friends and relatives she had left behind. We wondered if she would long for the many toys she had been stockpiling for the first five years of her life. We were also concerned that if we stayed in the U.S., the American way would be deeply ingrained in her young mind, and she wouldn't be happy in a country where compromises, concessions, and outright sacrifices are a part of daily survival.

SierraSky loved living in Belize as much as we did. We found that she could easily live without the Wal-Mart-type stores and drive-thru restaurants. Her needs became simple and she seemed quite content with her beautiful surroundings and bevy of Belizean playmates. Of the five of us, SierraSky had the toughest start on the island. The day after we arrived here she reported that her tooth fell apart. We were shocked! It appeared that her expensive resin filling had cracked and fallen out. We took her to the local clinic which is provided by the government of Belize. After a reasonable wait, a very kind dentist and oral surgeon named Dr. Cima took us into his ultra-modern office. He did a thorough exam and reported that not only did her filling fall out, but the cavity had grown during the time it had loosened from the tooth. It looked as though she was going to need a root canal, including a crown, if the tooth was going to last until she is twelve. That wasn't the only surprise. We found out that the examination was free! That same evening, Dr. Cima worked on her mouth in his own clinic on Middle Street for over an hour. SierraSky was a total trooper during what is normally a tedious and painful procedure.

Our concerns about SierraSky were quickly dissolved. Since her first day here, she was surrounded by happy little San Pedranos. When we showed up to look at our new apartment, the neighborhood children discovered us waiting patiently for the landlord in the front yard. SierraSky made friends with kids who are still her best friends today.

One of the first girls that SierraSky befriended was named Joyce-Marie Martinez. She is the daughter of the local elementary school's principal, Miss Addy. SierraSky was going to start school for the first time and "Isla Bonita Elementary School" was the logical choice. Joyce-Marie was SierraSky's best buddy. They would walk to school holding each other's hands every day. The sight of them in their maroon and khaki school uniforms was darling.

We threw a "half-birthday" party for SierraSky when she turned five and-a-half. Six of her new friends accompanied her to the huge pool at the Fitness Center for fun and games. Later, they came to our house for cake and ice cream. Everybody wore party hats and the day was a big hit. They had never heard of a "half-birthday party" and they were easily convinced to celebrate it with her!

Other than special parties, the kids spent their days playing outside, going to the beach, taking walks to the park, and making leaf and sand soup. They were excited when SierraSky would receive mail from the States which included toys, shiny new fun items, and even some USD.

Children in Belize are well behaved for the most part. They have respect for people and property. This is taught to them at an early age and they recognize the value of things. They are not as spoiled as the youth in America. Generally speaking, you will not find boxes full of toys, expensive video games, or televisions in kid's bedrooms.

The parents are quite strict and usually there are extended family members around who help discipline the kids. Children have a place of importance in this culture and the 2010 census determined that 58% of the island's population is under 24 years of age.

The adults here are very playful. They somehow manage to maintain their inner child in spite of hardship caused by high unemployment on the island. Grown men laugh and tease and joke with each other. Anything that is fun to do comes easily to the good humored Belizeans. The sound of genuine laughter is everywhere it seems, with most of it coming from the happy children that live here. This is a great place for raising a healthy child.

"The thing that impresses me the most about America is the way parents obey their children."

King Edward VIII

Chapter 12

AT LAST...A TRIP TO THE REEF

There are times in life when you just have to seize the opportunity to go out and get what you want. Three months after moving to San Pedro we finally took the time to get in a boat and go out to the reef! It's easy to keep busy in our day-to-day lives, and put off the things that we really love. I have decided that visiting the sea is the one thing that I love most about living on this island. You must take the time to sail over the turquoise water and glide along the coral in a sixteen foot skiff, admiring the crashing waves and breath-taking beauty of the seemingly endless reef. It stimulates the mind and body, and elevates the five senses. You tend to feel exceptionally alive and invigorated! Its sheer magnitude humbles us, as we began to realize what tiny creatures we are, and the whole experience makes our problems seem somewhat insignificant. Almost every guest on the island comes to visit the reef, for diving, fishing, or snorkeling. Once you have been out there...you can't wait to do it again! Each day is different. On some days there is a big white line where the waves are breaking against the coral barrier. Other days the reef is un-discernible because the sea is calm.

One day I woke up and looked out over the water while enjoying my tea and morning meditation and I said to myself "Today is the day!" It was sunny, calm and hot. The sky was a deep shade of blue and there were white puffy clouds rolling by. I went to Jo-mama and Cindi's house and said "Let's go out on the glass bottom boat, the perfect day for it is finally here." Jo was excited. She longed to hop into a boat and get closer to the white line of waves that beckons to everyone who visits here. When you look out over the sea day after day, it calls to you, draws you nearer, and tempts you to come out and explore its mysteries!

After waiting patiently for twelve weeks, nothing compared to the feeling of floating in a glass-bottom boat and gently cruising the short distance to the reef. It is about a 1/2 mile east of the island. Many Belizeans take kayaks, canoes, or even take a risky swim to reach it. The reef is easily accessed by everyone.

Unfortunately, Cindy wasn't home from shopping in time to join us. Robert chose to hang back and wait for the kids to come home from school, fix their snacks and guide the homework process. This day's brave sailors would include Jo-mama and me, and Captain "Chicho" and his family.

In about a half an hour we arrived at Hol Chan Marine Park and National Reserve. This was a very new concept for me. A "park" in the water. It is a protected area of the sea where no one can fish, spear, or harass the marine life in any manner. Strict penalties are enforced for those who don't respect the Belizean laws. It is an area of the reef where an incredible array of tropical fish gather around the coral to feed, make their homes, and reproduce.

It was a pleasant surprise when the boat captain encouraged us to swim even though it wasn't a typical dive boat. Nurse sharks come right up to you as you swim around, and show no fear of humans. It is a thrill to touch them as they slowly pass next to you! They are basically harmless and universally recognized as a non-aggressive species of shark.

Jo-mama chose not to swim that day. She was fascinated by viewing the fish and coral through the glass bottom of the boat. There were jack mackerel, Spanish mackerel, sting rays, eagle rays, grouper, blue tangs, yellow snapper, and even an occasional sea turtle. I was leery of the five foot barracuda swimming among the schools of fish.

The colorful coral formations just below the surface are spectacular. You want to float above them in your snorkeling gear forever. I was brave enough to swim around in the coral all by myself. I saw rainbow fish that were so large, they truly looked like rainbows swimming along. I was a bit scared when I saw the 4 foot grouper hanging out under the neighboring boat. I got used to him as I swam around and observed him observing me.

As the sun began its descent in the sky, it was time to go back on board the glass-bottom cruiser and depart the beautiful underworld at the reef. To my delight, I found out that I could climb onto the roof of the boat and ride home with the sun and wind in my face. It was the best look-out perch that anyone could ask for. What a fabulous panoramic view. As we left the park I saw a fantastic eagle ray soar through the water. It was an unforgettable and exhilarating experience! I told my-self, "I must remember to do this again...as soon as possible."

"Many go fishing without knowing it is fish they are after."

Henry David Thoreau

Chapter 13

THE ISLAND IS NOT FOR EVERYONE

We were all very surprised by, and impressed with the adventurous spirit of Mr. John Brandley. He was the first person to come and visit us here in Belize. John and Jo-mama have been dating since SierraSky was born. We remember the day he stopped his car in the middle of the street in front of our home and said "I heard that there is a new baby in the house." Without even knowing that John and Jo-mama had recently become fast friends, Robert invited him in to see our newborn, SierraSky. He has been a part of the family ever since, bringing Jo to our home for frequent visits to see "the little sweetheart" during SierraSky's early years in Wisconsin.

John was interested in discovering the far-away foreign land that we constantly talked about before we moved our family to Latin America. I think what really called him to Belize was his loved ones. He said he couldn't believe how much SierraSky has changed in the three months since we had moved. It is amazing how fast a child develops and changes and absorbs things like a little sponge. She had grown taller and her hair was a little longer. She had picked-up a Belizean accent and had acquired a deep tan from all of the swimming and time spent on the beach with her new-found friends.

It was unlikely that John would be the first to come to visit us here in Belize. He is a very cautious man, careful with each decision he makes, scrupulous with his shillings, and not exactly a young buck anymore. He hadn't been on a plane in over a decade and the last time he flew out of the country was thirty years ago. Nothing could stop him. He came down here, one flight after another, and arrived in good spirits and reported, "It was a breeze! Much easier than I thought it would be."

John was very taken with the culture and the simple way of life here in San Pedro Town. I suggested to Robert that we show John around the island, but to be sure and keep him on Front Street where all the nice hotels beautify the beach, and the quaint little gift shops line the paved street. We didn't want to shock him by showing him the difficult circumstances that many island residents have to deal with every day.

John had other plans. He wanted to see every bit of the island. We inevitably ended up on bustling Middle Street and on the lagoon-side that locals refer to as Back Street. This is where the local food stands, delis, markets, fisherman's wharf, and boat docks are. It is a little dustier and a bit more run-down. The extra wide Back Street makes up for the extra narrow Middle Street where the taxi's and golf carts precariously share a single lane with the bicycle riders and pedestrians. It is more like an alley than a main thoroughfare. It is a good thing they made it a one-way street. It couldn't support any more traffic than it already does.

What John enjoyed most was observing how the local San Pedranos live and how they meet their daily needs. He was amazed at how happy even the poorest people appeared to be.

We were surprised that John decided to come to Belize and were pleased that he appreciated the "third world" aspect of the island. He is a very neat and meticulous man, finding perfection and security in things being just right, safe, and clean. It was an incongruity for him to enjoy spending hours in the golf cart touring the less privileged neighborhoods. It didn't seem to be in standing with his usual inclinations. He said "I am just fascinated at how they live here, so simply, and how they are able to provide for their families without having much income, and yet they appear very happy. I don't see anyone living without the basic necessities. Very few people act like they are living in rough conditions. Once you start talking with them, you find out that they feel the richest of all."

Our next-door neighbor Tino is a renowned fisherman on the island and very popular with tourists who come here to fish.

Handsome, healthy, and strong, he has a wonderful family that he takes very good care of. Early one afternoon when he returned from a fishing excursion, he began to clean the 'catch' on his dock. The American tourist, who hired Tino's boat that morning, was talking to him as he gutted and scaled the snapper, grouper, and barracuda they had caught.

As the tourist collected his fish, he tucked $400 into Tino's pocket. The man asked him if he would like to go out and fish later in the day, as he had some friends who would pay $500 for a great fishing trip like he just had. Smiling, Captain Tino politely refused his offer. He was headed home to his wife and children who were waiting on the front porch for him. His client said, "Don't be foolish friend. You can make more than twice the money you expected today. You could save some money and one-day get another boat and make even more. Someday you will have a fleet of fishing boats and you could retire and relax all day long." Tino smiled as he replied, "The things that you wish for me, I already have, and I am happy. Thank you for your kind offer."

It is a common belief in Belize that the poor man has a richer life. Here they understand that wealth does not bring happiness. The love of family and friends, and time spent with them is much more important than money.

We were starting to piece together how a whole society could be so content in life. They were never taught that they needed so many "things" to be satisfied. Of course not every single one of them is walking on clouds all of the time, but they are generally happier and less stressed-out than Americans. The Belizeans are very approachable. Everyone waves to each other and says "hello" with a smile. If you stop to talk, they will take the time and have a nice chat with you. Conversations with strangers are usually polite, relaxed and can be lengthy. It is a rare sight, and definitely out of place to see someone rushing or being hasty. Maybe it is the sunshine, the ever-present shades of blue and green, or the feeling of security from knowing that family and relatives are nearby that makes these people so at ease! Whatever it is, John Brandley noticed it, and he loved it too.

One of John's favorite parts of the trip was when we were invited to SierraSky's friend Shannon's first communion party. He was made to feel welcome by the Belizean family and invited to take part in their joy. Eight year old Shannon Nunez looked so pretty in her special dress that day and the kids had a lot of fun playing soccer or "futbol" in their sandy yard. It seemed more like a contest to see who could get their Sunday clothes the dirtiest! SierraSky was glad to be there for the fun and the beautiful homemade cake, of course. The food this family served to us was delicious. We were inspired to learn the unusual names and recipes of these wonderful taste-treats.

The biggest surprise of all was when Jo-mama announced that she would be going back to the States with John. It was a tough decision and she struggled with her choice right up to the last minute. She missed her family in Wisconsin, but if she returned to them, she would miss her family here in Belize.

Ultimately, it was the conveniences of the States that swayed her decision to leave us, the warmth, the sea, and the palm trees. For an eighty-two year old who has suffered a stroke, it is necessary to have first-rate medical services available, concrete under foot instead of sand, cushioned chairs instead of wooden or bamboo furniture, a car instead of a golf cart, Burger King instead of open-food stands, and of course, the millions of amenities that big, bad ol' Wal-mart offers. . . San Pedro Town is not for everyone. You can be young-at-heart, but it helps to be young in years and relatively good health to live comfortably on the island.

Jo-mama and her best friend John went home to Wisconsin where a fresh foot of snow had just fallen during their flight back. We hope they will visit us again one day and we look forward to their return.

"Honest differences are often a healthy sign of progress."

Mahatma Gandhi

Chapter 14

THE HOLIDAYS

Belize has thirteen national holidays and Belizeans make the best of each one! There are twelve holidays in the United States that are celebrated here for the tourists and the ex-patriots. There is a significant Canadian population here, and they bring another thirteen national holidays with them. This country celebrates thirty-eight holidays a year. That is more than three parties per month. Sound like a good time? On top of that there are numerous religious holidays celebrated by the various sects.

It seems as though every major religion is represented on the island. Belize is forty percent Catholic and in this part of the world the Catholic's tend to dominate the news. Here in San Pedro there is religious tolerance and you will find many houses of worship built by Baptists, Lutherans, Protestants, Muslims, Hindi's,

Jehovah's Witnesses, Seventh Day Adventists, Mormons, Mennonites, born-again Christians, Anglicans, Episcopalians, and Buddhists. There are even a few Jewish residents on the island. Everyone seems to get along quite well. When you are surrounded by sunshine and blue skies and palm trees, it is hard to be upset about much at all. Religious or political differences don't seem to affect the camaraderie here on Isla Bonita.

We have had the pleasure of experiencing many holidays in Belize. What we eventually found out is that Belize actually recognizes (in the neighborhood of) 70 holidays and festivals every year. And don't forget everyone's birthday which is celebrated with great fervor, and with extreme festivities that usually include a few days off of work to recover. Halloween, St. Valentines' Day, and even St. Patrick's Day are enough of a reason for Belize to throw a big party.

There are week-long celebrations like the San Pedro Carnival, Cocoa Festival, Sugar-Cane Festival, San Pedro Days, Lobster Festival, Costa Maya Festival, Cashew Festival, Coconut Festival,

Dia de San Pedro, Deer Dance Festival, International Sea and Air Festival, Mexican National Day, and at least ten more annual celebrations that cannot be ignored if you live around here. They just don't quit finding ways to have the most fun you can have in Belize. It will wear you out if you try to hit every party, so go slow and take it easy!

The thirteen Belizean holidays are:

New Year's Day (January 1st and 2nd!)

Baron Bliss Day, also known as National Heroes and Benefactors Day (March 9th) D. Baron Bliss bequeathed his fortune (2 million USD) to the people of British Honduras (Belize's previous name) in 1926. The trust has helped Belize in countless ways!

Good Friday (calculated by church calendar)

Holy Saturday

Easter Sunday (the most important religious holiday, it runs from Wednesday through Monday)

Labour Day (May 1st) A day to celebrate the workers in Belize.

Sovereign's Day/Commonwealth Day (May 21st) Honoring the Queen of England and Belize being accepted into the Commonwealth.

St. Georges Caye Day (September 10th) Remembering the "Baymen" who battled the Spanish in 1798, and won the rights to this land we call Belize.

Independence day (September 21st) Commemorating Belize's independence from British Colonial rule in 1981. The biggest celebration in Belize!

10.) Pan American Day (October 11th) A celebration of all things

Latin American.

11.) Garifuna Settlement Day (November 19th) Celebrates the arrival of the Garifuna in Belize with the exception of indigenous Mayans.

12.) Christmas day (December 25th)

13.) Boxing Day (December 26th) The Belizeans are smart and throw in an extra holiday the day after Christmas to nurse their hangovers. Just kidding! Boxing Day is traditionally a day following Christmas when people in the United Kingdom would box up their presents.

Our first holiday to participate in was Garifuna Day, November 19th. This is a celebration of the discovery of Belize by the African slaves who were released from captivity when the slave-ships that brought them here crashed on the reef. The English slave traders un-locked their shackles rather than let them perish in the wreck, hoping to recapture them later and sell them at auction for large sums of gold and silver. Many swam to shore in the storms and were never found by their captors. They never worked as slaves and are very proud of this in their historical record.

The Garifuna are a significant percentage of the population here in Belize. Their skin tone is very dark from their African fore-fathers. Many wear their hair in dreadlocks and they prefer bright, colorful clothing. They cook delicious meals from recipes handed down for generations, that include beans, rice, corn, and lots of spicy meats. Garifuna foods are unique and very tasty!

The celebration that morning started with a re-enactment of the discovery of the Belizean shoreline at the first light of dawn. The actors rowed their boats to shore at central park. Then there was lively, traditional dances performed around town by the Garifunas who were dressed in African style dresses and costumes. A twenty-four hour drumming circle was the constant rhythmic background on this day. It was an exciting event for us. We had only been on the island for ten days and we were still getting to know our new surroundings.

Shortly after Garifuna Day was Thanksgiving. We enjoyed a mouth-watering meal of lobster, shrimp, and spotted grouper with coconut cream sauce for dinner at Ramon's Village. This resort is a group of little villas with palapa rooftops. The restaurant and pool area has one enormous palapa over-head, reaching about 50 ft. high! The back wall of the restaurant is a gigantic sculpture of a Mayan god with typical facial features such as the high cheekbones and sharp nose. It was a bit distracting having such a sculpture watching over us as we ate. The first Thanksgiving that we enjoyed on the island will be remembered for a long time to come. "More lobster, please!"

Christmas was lovely. There is nothing than compares to seeing the palm trees wrapped in festive Christmas tree lights! This was our first Christmas that we spent watching a lighted boat parade contest instead of watching a wintery cold parade in the snow. We yelled and cheered for the catamaran with the drumming band on it. We found out later that it won the contest and that it was the kids from SierraSky's school who were on that boat. Jo-mama bought a bushy little plant with a large number of red blooms on it to decorate their house. Our neighbor Robert, the guitar player from Alabama, gave us a little tree to decorate and put SierraSky's gifts under. We also celebrated Chanukah by lighting the menorah each night. SierraSky is getting to see all sides of life, Christian, Jewish, Belizean and many others...

The New Year's celebration was a blast! We danced to the music of Dennis Wolfe and the Usual Suspects as they played on the beach at BC's bar. This palapa-bar, located right by the sea, is a destination for many tourists. BC's is where we have made friends with ex-patriots who have moved here from the United States and Canada. Hundreds of gringos have happily left the land of "too many rules" and moved to Belize.

We celebrated New Years Eve with these free-spirited folks as we listened to the romantic music on the beach under the bright light of a full moon. Our new friends from Canada, Lorna "Cookie" and Gordon taught us how to Texas two-step. Robert tried not to step on her toes too many times as Lorna patiently taught him the cowboy dance he'd wanted to learn for thirty years. Sometimes you have to come to a tropical island to learn how to dance in Texas! A 'thank you' kiss was stolen at mid-night from Cookie, and Robert hoped this didn't step on Gordon's toes. We danced late into the night at the warm water's edge, surrounded by a billion twinkling stars. It was a fantastic way to bring in the New Year!

St. Valentine's Day was a real treat. The school had a beauty contest and the kids dressed up in their finest Valentine-type clothing that day. Sierrasky wore a pretty red dress with gold trim and our neighbor Griselda helped with her fingernail painting and hairstyling. SierraSky and Joyce-Marie each won first place in their class and SierraSky won 1st-place for the whole school. First-prize was $100. We were astounded when she won!

The next big festival was Carnaval. This is borrowed from the Brazilian holiday that is the prelude to Lent. It is the party that peaks on Fat Tuesday, before starting the 40 day fasting period on Ash Wednesday. I always wanted to go to Mardi Gras, otherwise known as "Carnaval" in Latin America.

"The foolish man seeks happiness in the distance, the wise grows it under his feet."

James Oppenheim I

Chapter 15

CARNAVAL

San Pedro Town loves to throw a party! I couldn't wait to see what this holiday would be like. The first night of Carnaval opened with The Dance Company's spectacular performance in Central Park. Group after group of dancers performed in traditional bright ethnic costumes until 11:00 pm! SierraSky's friends Shannon and Jessica were stars of the show and looked so grown up in their extremely ornate dresses. The celebration lasted so long that SierraSky fell asleep on our laps long before we called it a night.

Have you heard the expression "Let's paint the town red?" Well, on this island they mean it literally! On Sunday, the first day of Carnaval, the younger kids run through the streets and throw paint on each other. Yes, real paint! The next day is when grown men dress as women and dance in a conga line up and down the streets into the wee hours. These "man-girls" dance in front of local businesses and solicit money which is given to local charities. It's hilarious to watch!

On Fat Tuesday, anyone near the beach or Central Park is fair game for having paint thrown at them. The locals call this "getting painted." Thankfully, everybody uses water-based paints. The painted victims jump into the sea after the fun is over, to scrub and bathe, using a little sand to coax the paint off of their skin . . .

Another tradition on the island is dressing up in costumes. People make elaborate costumes such as fairies with wings and ugly cockroaches. There is a special dance they do where they try to catch and "kill" the cockroach. There are all kinds of people donned in hand-made creative costumes that stretch the imagination. Groups dance through the streets for tips and then disperse the money to the needy at the end of the night. Locals refer to this as "comparsa" and it is another long-lived carnaval tradition.

We didn't let SierraSky get painted during the craziness of Fat Tuesday. We drove the kids around in our golf cart and took photos. Our neighbors told us that if we were in the golf cart we would be safe. We would look like tourists and they wouldn't paint us. We dressed the kids in costumes for our drive through San Pedro Town. I tried to get the girls to dress as men and the boys to dress as ladies, but they refused. They were adorable in their make-shift costumes anyway.

When we returned from observing the craziness downtown, the kids were begging to paint each other. We didn't want them playing with the messy paint, and they were very disappointed. Griselda had the idea to use baby powder and flour instead. The kids had a ball chasing each other around the yard and throwing powder. It was such fun, and an easy clean-up.

We were not the only ones who were leery of the paint throwing. There were many letters to the editor of the San Pedro Sun the following week expressing great disapproval. Many people resent the destructive behavior. They have suggested that in the future, we may confine everyone who wants to paint each other to the futbol field. It makes sense to me. We'll see what next year's Carnaval has in store for us. I'm sure it will be loads of fun for everyone.

"A smile will gain you ten more years of life."

Chinese proverb

Chapter 16

STAMPING PASSPORTS

Belize discourages people from purchasing a one-way airline ticket to their country. You must purchase a round-trip ticket unless you have residency or citizenship in Belize, or other special exceptions such as a work or school permit. If you are able to purchase a one-way ticket, it is because the travel agent or travel website missed the technicality and you got lucky. Once you arrive, you are allowed a 30 day stay in Belize. When your one-month visa expires, all visitors to Belize are required to go to the Immigration and Nationality Department and pay $50 Belize ($25 USD) to request a visa extension stamp in their passport. Each extension allows you to remain in Belize 30 days. After six months, the fee goes up to $100.00 BZD. If you live here, and are in school, you can request and purchase a student permit and it replaces the need for monthly stamping. It costs $50BZD and is valid for the school year which can be as long as ten months. A valid work-permit also replaces the requirement for a monthly stamp. If you acquire a work permit which costs $1000 USD it is only valid for one year and must be renewed upon expiration.

Another option for remaining in Belize without monthly stamping, a work permit or a student permit is to apply for the Qualified Retired Persons Incentives Act (QRP). If you can prove that you have adequate funds(at least $2,000 USD per month, per adult) to survive in Belize without working here or taking money out of the community, you can apply for your residency with the QRP right away. If you choose this route you are not allowed to work at all. We decided that the QRP program would not benefit us, and that earning a living on the island was definitely in our future.

We were told that the work permit application process can take from six months to two years! We also heard that you can speed up this procedure by "expediting" it through "someone" who has connections in Belmopan, the capital city of Belize and the seat of the Belizean governing party. It is the "someone" part that can be tricky. You have to pay the right person or your mistake can come back to haunt you. More particularly, the officers from the Immigration and Nationality Department can arrest you and put you in jail for working without a valid work permit. That's when you find out you paid the wrong person. We decided to go with the long-term plan and follow proper legal procedures. We found ourselves in the enviable position of not being able to go to work right away, even if we wanted to.

We learned about most of this from local ex-pat's who enjoyed talking about their experiences. At first we were a bit wary of the Immigration officers because of the stories we had heard.

It is typical for Americans to come down to Belize and not have an immediate grasp of the relaxed demeanor of Belizeans. To our Belizean hosts, we generally appear to be a bit hasty, sometimes impolite and loud, and all too often, just plain rude! This attitude can cause the local workers to stereotype us as demanding and impatient. Their natural reaction is to be less than friendly or helpful in situations that may help us to prolong our stay in Belize. Many foreigners come here thinking they somehow *deserve* the right to be in this country, and therefore show very little respect or gratitude for the privilege of staying in Belize.

Robert was quick to recognize the fact that the Immigration officers are people just like us, with families to support and jobs to do. He spoke to them with respect. He also addressed them as though he was talking to a friend, asking them how their kids are, how their day was going, etc. Then he would proceed with the technical questions that we began to have. The officers were very kind and willing to help us, and not the stern and indifferent people that they had been made out to be by many Ex-pat's. We have since adopted the attitude that no matter how long we live in Belize, we will always be humble guests in this beautiful country and this attitude has worked out well for us. Although the officers can be a bit terse with the loud and demanding gringos, Belizean people are the friendliest in the Caribbean when respect is shown toward them. We try to keep in mind that Caucasians are in the minority here. We are pretty easy to spot in a crowd. It is important to us, as un-official ambassadors from America, to be on our best behavior at all times.

I regret that we didn't ask the Immigration and Nationality Department about the work permit process sooner than we did. Our reticence to deal with local authorities was unfounded. They were very helpful to us during all of our dealings with them. We live, and we learn.

"You can't catch a cub without going into the tiger's den."
Chinese proverb

Chapter 17

HAMMOCKS AND THE CARIBBEAN GO HAND IN HAND

There is some special connection between hammocks and the West Indies. They just go hand in hand. I don't know the history of it, but I have noticed that palm trees seem to grow perfectly spaced for hanging a hammock from one tree to the other. Nature has great instincts.

I had always wanted a good hammock and one day I finally made the investment. At first I was looking at one for $250 USD. It was the deluxe model, quite large, with finely woven silky threads, top-of-the-line styling, extra support, and very comfortable. Instead I decided on one for twenty five dollars and was happy with it. So happy, in fact, that I bought a second one just like it! Once we figured out how to hang it securely, I climbed in and didn't want to get back out. I noticed from then on, that whenever I would take a moment to relax, it would turn into a lengthy, dreamy experience, which almost always included my favorite book of the day. This addition to our homestead brought me one step closer to understanding the happy, relaxed, contented demeanor of the Belizeans.

When Robert and I hung the hammocks in our back patio area, it was like adding a new room to our house, possibly the best room of all. We set up a few deck chairs, hung some new clothes lines, and bought a little barbeque grill and a mahogany table to serve lunch on.

The floor of the patio area was maroon cobblestone and majestic white pillars held up the third floor apartment. A variety of trees outlined the edges of the property. These acted as a buffer zone to the neighboring buildings. The bougainvillea was interspersed among the coconut palms, ficus, and banana trees. The hibiscus tree, which is eight feet tall, was full of fresh blooms every day. The schefflera tree was over two stories tall. This is a plant that I had in my house back in Wisconsin. Mine was a whopping two feet tall. I also had a ficus tree on our front porch in the States, that was only four feet tall and I was pretty proud of it. The ficus trees that edged our patio were easily ten feet high. As an avid gardener, I found this very exciting! I had no idea how big these 'houseplants' could grow in their natural outdoor environment. It is such a lovely experience living in a place where the trees and flowers grow so easily with very little care.

"A book is like a garden carried in the pocket"

Chinese proverb

Chapter 18

A Day in the Life of Robert, Lydia, and SierraSky

Fortunately for us, we had sold a part of our business before moving from the States, and this afforded us the time to watch and learn about the "island way of life." For the first few months, I spent a lot of time lounging in the hammock, catching up on my reading, marveling at the sea, watching boats go out, watching boats come in, sipping fresh coconut juice, eating almonds from the tree in our front yard, and enjoying a daily swim! I also spent my time writing about our new life here on the island. Aside from all of this relaxing, we somehow managed to keep busy every day. Isn't it amazing how life, and just plain living, takes so much time and effort? Of course I can't include everything here, but here is how we would spend a typical day . . .

At around 6:00 am the sun would come streaming in our bedroom windows and wake us up. It was very bright and it shone right through our blinds and curtains. We would get up at sunrise. At 5:00 am it would still be cool in our room from the breeze during the night, but by 8:00 am it would start to get very warm. 6:00 am was the perfect time to get up and get going.

After I helped SierraSky brush her teeth, fix her hair, and get dressed in her school uniform she would run down the stairs and join Robert who had toast and cereal or eggs and pancakes with fresh fruit ready and waiting for her. More often than not, she was bright and chipper in the morning and a joy to be around! We would have to coax her to eat. She is much more interested in living life, than eating food. I don't know how some kids can have so much energy without eating much at all. I wish I knew her secret. After breakfast, she would grab her schoolbag and she and Robert would climb into the golf cart and cruise down the beach to pick up Joyce Marie.

The school kids in San Pedro have heavy back-packs because they must bring all of their books to and from school each day instead of leaving them behind in their desks. The bags are so heavy that they have to hunch forward just to keep them up. It is a common site to see a group of school kids walking like a pack of hunchbacks! To assist with the burden, we would give our daughter and her friends a ride. We would let them walk home for lunch because they could leave their bags at school during the noon-hour break.

Robert and I had some personal time from 8:15 until noon to do as we pleased. For the first several months we always had something that we wanted to do or see. Sometimes we would go shopping and pick up things we needed for our new homes.

Aunt Cindi and Jo-mama were invited on a little adventure each day to get them out of the house. Often, we would go to Caye Supply, the local small-scale version of WAL-mart and buy a cooking utensil or kitchen item that we found we couldn't live without. We had to discover what was available at various locations, and where to purchase items at the best price. We would frequent hardware stores, little outdoor Guatemalan markets with plastic products and brooms, and tiny little domestic-supply stores that you would never have noticed if someone hadn't told you to go there, and gave you specific directions how to find them.

It took a while to get both households functioning smoothly, but once we settled in, we were able to stay at home and do the things we've wanted to do for years. We finally had the time to delve into the many books we lugged down to Belize with us, and to play our guitars on a regular schedule. Reading and playing music are two of life's real luxuries. How nice to indulge in them!

Normally, the kids would show up at noon, hot and red-faced from their dusty walk in the mid-day sun and heat. We never knew how many were coming for lunch. The first thing they would ask was, "What's for lunch Mr. Robert?" Then they would enjoy fresh fruits and cheese, or hot-dogs and beans, or peanut butter and jelly with local sweet bananas. Joyce's grandmother "Chi- Chi" would send along something to share, such as more fruit, burritos, stew chicken or beans and rice. Joyce would always dive into her food and then ask, "What's the after-school snack (pronounced snahhhhk) Mr. Robert?" She knew that there would be something yummy in our kitchen at the end of the school day. We finally let them leave the lunch-table when we felt that SierraSky had eaten enough 'real food' to get her through the afternoon.

At 12:45 the kids would grab each other's hands and walk back to school together. Depending upon the day of the week we would have until either 2:00 or 3:00 pm all to ourselves. We would jump on our golf cart and drive around town doing errands like going to the beverage distribution center, Bowen & Bowen to re-fill our water jugs and purchase Beliken beer at wholesale prices. Then we would stop at a Guatemalan fruit stand to get some oranges, watermelon, bananas, mangos, soursop dragon-fruit, papaya, or a huge, fresh pineapple. So much delicious fruit…so little time!

We would include a drive by the fisherman's dock to see if there was any fresh snapper caught on that morning's excursions. Then we would swing by one of the Mennonite vegetable stands to get some potatoes, carrots, cucumbers, cabbage, onions, cilantro, romaine lettuce, broccoli and tomatoes. It was fun to buy fresh herbs and dried spices at the roadside booths to improve the flavor our home-cooked meals. Sometimes we would stop at Super-Buy, the local supermarket which is owned by our previous landlords. When you can't find the more specialized packaged items that are so common in the States, this is the store that will have it.

When the kids would come home after school, they were often eager to go swimming. First Robert would make ice-cold smoothies with an assortment of fresh fruits and we would have the kids do their homework while they enjoyed the treats. Then we would all get into our swimming suits and head down to the beach. I would usually let the girls swim in the shallow area for awhile and then we would go out to the end of the pier and jump in. Most of the Belizean children love to swim everyday and seem to have endless energy for it.

There are hundreds of colorful fish under the long-boat docks. It was a lot like swimming in an aquarium! Sometimes we would get a thrill as a three foot wide sting-ray swam past us. They are not dangerous unless you jump into the water right on top of one and startle it, or accidentally step on one in the shallows. We would always be sure to look carefully all around us before we would enter the water. It is best to be aware of your surroundings anytime you swim in the sea.

There is also a new threat to the reef in the coastal waters of Belize. It is called the lionfish. The lionfish recently arrived from Asian waters and they are prolific and a nuisance. They breed like mice and the population explosion is already taking a toll on the inhabitants of the reef. They can eat their own weight in fish every day. Lionfish are very poisonous, and if you are poked by their spines the toxins released can cause a severe allergic reaction, even life-threatening at times.

The environmental community here has recently implemented a lionfish catching contest. No one can wipe out a species better or faster than mankind, especially if the fishermen are competing for prizes! We haven't seen any lionfish close to shore yet. They have been caught on the reef quite frequently, and have a delicious flavor and texture. Their edibility should put their status in jeopardy on an island where a fish dinner is the favorite family dish.

After swimming around the man-made coral, and jumping off the pier over and over again, I would have to force the girls to head home.

The Belizean children love SierraSky and often tried to make our house their second home. It's not too bad, the more the merrier as long as they go home at sunset. Belizean children are very well behaved and SierraSky loved to have them as guests.

After dinner and some quality time together, we often go out to hear our favorite band at one of many little family bars on the beach. It is such a small island that we usually know people who are out with their kids. We would share stories with our new friends as we enjoyed the happy hour rum drink-special of the day and the kids built their sand castles in the shadows of the setting sun. There were always new and interesting people arriving on the island. It was fun to hear their stories from another land, and tell them about our experiences here on the island. We found that many tourists who visit Ambergris Caye would say they want to move here, just like we did.

Long days in the sun are filled with fresh air rolling in off of the vast sea. This makes it is easy to "call it a day" around nine pm. After tucking SierraSky into bed for the night and promising to "see her in dreamland," we would often take a moment on our balcony to welcome the cool night, and watch the moon and stars rise over the water.

On many occasions we would see interesting lights in the sky. We brought a pair of binoculars but we wished we had brought our telescope to Belize. The stars look very different down here. I do not recognize the constellations like I used to, and the moon rises and sets in a new place in the sky. We have seen the Southern Cross and it is spectacular! Robert thinks it's a regular UFO circus in our night sky, and that Belize must be their favorite playground! We need that telescope down here to make a proper evaluation of the strange lights in the sky that we would see on a regular basis. They are not satellites.

When weather permits, we would fall asleep with our windows open-wide to enjoy the sea breezes that would blow right through the house and cool everything off from the heat of the day. Then it was off to dreamland...and the promise of another beautiful, sunny, warm day in paradise.

"An inch of time is an inch of gold but you can't buy that inch of time with an inch of gold."

Chinese proverb

Chapter 19

PARADISE UPGRADED!

If someone had told me that we were going to move out of our beloved apartment near the sea, I would have laughed out loud and then become worried and upset. I am sure that's how Robert felt when I told him that we were going to move right away! He loved our home and the people we shared the building with. I announced that we would be moving in two days, on his birthday, and to "Please trust me, this will be the best birthday present you ever had."

Robert appreciated our apartment at the Emerald Reef Suites. He enjoyed the view, the porch open to the street, the iguana outside in the ficus tree, and most of all he loved our neighbors who shared the building with us. Mr. Enrique, our landlord, and Miss Cindy, his daughter, were very kind to us and became our friends over the four months that we shared their building. Miss Monica who lived upstairs, was always a delight to bump into and have a long deep conversation with. Big Bob and Berta-Lydia across the hall were like room-mates to us. Robert and Big Bob had many late-night spontaneous guitar sessions. As a rule, unplanned musical moments are usually the best. Robert was already missing our friends before we even moved. Life is change, and it's only natural to resist it.

Now this is how it all came together. I was strolling along the beach one day on my usual route up the sandy lane called Boca del Rio drive. I looked up and spotted a "For Rent" sign on my favorite beach-house. It was called La Casita and it had the biggest yard on the beach. I was sure it would be unaffordable for us but I asked about it anyway. To my surprise, the price had just been lowered because of tough times in the global economy. It was only a little bit more than we were currently paying for our apartment. I had always lived in a large house, never an apartment, and it was an adjustment for me to downsize. Oh! To have a whole house to ourselves again instead of a two-room flat. I had a new appreciation for what I once took for granted.

SierraSky was sad when she heard we were moving but as soon as she saw the new place, she quickly forgot about the old one. Robert can be stubborn and he didn't want to move. He didn't want the responsibility of taking care of a whole house again, but he did like the fact that it was right on the beach. The old saying goes: "No gamble, no gain." I am so happy that we took the risk, and the result has been much better than we could have imagined.

The most exciting part about the new house rental for me was the yard space available. There are very few properties on the beach that have a large front yard. I wanted to live on the beach where we could look out our windows and enjoy the splendor of the sea and all of its majesty, but on top of that, with my latest career idea that was dancing in my head, I needed an empty lot. . .

"A good fortune may forbode a bad luck, which may in turn disguise a good fortune."

Chinese proverb

Chapter 20

THE FIRST NEW CAREER PLAN

I was seriously thinking about what to do for my next career. I knew that I was not really interested in more work with pets and pet nutrition. I wanted to do something with plants and gardening. Caring for a garden is work that I have truly enjoyed throughout my life. I kept looking at the vast empty space that was our new front yard...

Most of the accessible land on the island is very sandy, and the best agricultural land is on the mainland. We love it so much here on the island, I dismissed the possibility of farming or gardening on a large scale. Moving to the mainland was out of the question.

We began to miss having herbs and vegetables growing right outside our door. We tried to purchase some rich black soil, but no one had any. Then we set out to buy some seedlings, such as basil, peppers or tomatoes, and nobody had any of those either. There wasn't a nursery on the island to purchase the most basic things needed for a small garden. The only plant related business that we heard about was closing down. The man who owned it had just passed away. I wondered, could this be opportunity knocking?

During our third month on the island I began to get a little stir-crazy and started to miss having something to keep me busy. I was elated when I finally made my decision. My next career would be establishing and operating a nursery! I loved plants, and I dreamed about buying and selling them. I could offer everything from vegetables to aloe, from flowers to cacti. I had made my decision and I began looking for an inexpensive yard to rent when I accidentally stumbled upon what would become our next home. I clearly saw my vision. I would have plants for sale in our huge front yard, and they could be displayed in such a way that it would look like a botanical garden! I began to plan how we would make this happen.

"The longer the night lasts, the more our dreams will be."

Chinese proverb

Chapter 21

ANOTHER TEAM-MATE RETURNS TO THE STATES

It was a sad day indeed when SierraSky's Aunt "Ninny" announced that she was returning to the United States! She told us, "This was the hardest decision I have ever made."

It's not very easy to find work in San Pedro Town. Making money in the USA is somewhat easier for a professional caregiver than it is in Belize because of cultural differences. Cindi was trained and accredited as a Waldorf school teacher, and is an expert in the care-giving profession. Here in Belize, and especially in the Latino culture, the young care for the old and feeble. Families take care of relatives with disabilities. There aren't any nursing homes or schools for the handicapped. It is all done by family members or friends. There was no work in her chosen profession here on Ambergris Caye.

Cindi has enjoyed many visits to the Caribbean, and has always dreamed of living where the pace of life was slower and more relaxed. She loved the sea outside her front door and the mild winter weather in San Pedro. She is a busy person and devoted a lot of her time helping with the Island Christmas in the Park and leading the singing of Christmas carols with the little Belizean children.

She volunteered at Isla Bonita Elementary School as a substitute teacher and the kids loved her! Unfortunately, there were no job openings for a full-time teacher because there were plenty of Belizeans available for the position. When the first Broadway play ever presented on the island came together for Valentine's Day, she volunteered as a drama and vocal coach. She did a splendid job teaching the high-school aged actors how to sing in Fiddler on the Roof with Dr. Floyd Jackson.

I believe that Cindi's greatest gift and talent is her ability to relate to, and teach young children. She is in her element when she is leading a group of kids through an art project or teaching them a new song and everyone is having a great time.   SierraSky was fortunate to have her "Aunt Ninny" close by in Wisconsin, and be able to spend the first six years of her life with her.

Although Cindi has always taught "that where there is the will, there is a way" it would have taken quite a bit of time and money to develop a successful plan that would enable her to stay on the island long term. I sensed that the island was not quite right for her at this time in her life, and she knew that she was needed back home.

Cindi is one of the most natural, organic people I have ever known.

She would always try to buy the organically grown food if the option was available. Whenever possible, she would use nature-friendly cleansers and all-natural baby powders and health products. She hated the concept of WAL-mart and the effect that it has on small local businesses and loved leaving it and all behind. After two months in San Pedro, Cindi mentioned some of her observations of the island to me. She was questioning whether the trade off was worth it, the warm weather for the lack of comforts and conveniences.

It was surprising to us when she discovered she missed the availability and selection that WAL-mart and other franchises provided. It is amazing how we had become so accustomed to these super-centers. We were used to going out and buying whatever we wanted, anything and everything under the sun at a one-stop shop for pennies! Living on an island gives you a new appreciation for that. Most goods and services are imported, and this raises the cost of everything you buy. Usually, the selection of products is very limited. We purchase what's available to us, and when we cannot find the item that is desired, we bite the bullet!

Another thing we didn't expect was what life would be like without a car for Cindi and Jo-mama. Just climbing onto the cart was difficult and bouncing around the streets can be quite taxing on the body. In the States we take it for granted when we hop into our comfortable cars and cruise over to the store or a drive-through restaurant. Can you imagine walking everywhere you had to go? Hiking on foot to the bank, the store, the post office, and Laundromat? This is more challenging for some people, especially when it is consistently hot, humid, and windy!

It is never too late in life to find something new and right for you. Life is full of opportunities if you are open to them and are willing to take a risk. Ultimately, it was with much trepidation and sadness that Aunt Ninny had to say good-bye for now to her little "pumpkin bumpkin" and set her compass for the United States. For as long as I live, I will never forget that morning when Aunt Ninny had to go to the local airport and board the island-hopper to the International Airport. It was truly a Sad Day of departure.

With the help of technology, we keep in touch with frequent emails, phone calls, and yearly visits from Cindi. Whenever we pass by the beach house that Cindi and Jo-mama lived in, we will remember it as "Cindi and Jo's place!"

"The journey is the reward."

Chinese Proverb

Chapter 22

SHARING THE ISLAND WITH OUR AMERICAN FRIENDS

We have met hundreds of new people here in San Pedro Town and many have become our friends. They have welcomed us by sharing their beliefs, personal thoughts, laughter, and this beautiful island. It's fun to get to know them, but this can make you miss your old friends even more.

In late March we had friends from the United States come to visit us for a week and we had a blast! There is something special about spending time in Belize with companions from back home. When you come from a typical Wisconsin background, you come with a Midwest point of view, and therefore, you see the island through similar eyes.

Tina and Jeff had been here before. In fact, Tina had once owned property here. With very little advance notice, the email came informing us that they were arriving soon and wondering if we needed anything from the States. There are so many things that we can't get here, the list became a long one, rather quickly. Tina is very thoughtful and generous. She has been to the island countless times managing her dance-student foreign exchange program. She knows first-hand that you won't find your favorite shampoo on the shelves in San Pedro stores!

Christina and Jeffrey came down here with destinations in mind that they had visited on previous trips and they looked forward to sharing them with us. We were all for it. You can count on us to volunteer to help our guests get their vacations rolling!

After a long day in planes and airports, most people work up an appetite. After landing on the island, it's time for food and drinks. They took us directly to a restaurant we had never been to called "El Fugon" which means 'the kettle'. The food is prepared Belizean style in the "old way." They cook big kettles of delicious side dishes by simmering them on open fires over hot coals. It was absolutely fabulous cuisine, and a real Belizean food experience. We enjoyed whole-snapper with beans and rice, and conch fritters that were good enough to die for! Suzanna, the woman who owns the restaurant, is a close friend of Tina's. She is a hard-worker, street-smart, and a very strong individual. Women often own and operate the successful businesses in Belize.

After our unique dining experience, we headed down to BC's cantina on the seashore, and enjoyed luscious tropical drinks and good conversation as we caught up on what was happening back home. We enjoyed live music as we listened to a local R&B singer named "TP" sing her heart out.

After the long day it was time to rest. The next morning we all piled into the golf cart and headed up north on an island-style road trip. Our first stop was the Palapa Bar which is a second-story bar at the end of a pier. The food is exceptional. The views from the bar are amazing, and you want to stay there all afternoon and just gaze at the sea. Since there were so many other great spots to eat and drink ahead of us, we forced ourselves to continue on.

We went to Ak' Bol, a yoga retreat and youth hostel-style hotel with beautiful cabanas on the beach. It is a peaceful respite from the noise and activity of San Pedro Town. The yoga sessions are held at the end of their long-boat dock at 6am. There is beautiful deck over the sea under a huge palapa that shades and protects you from sudden downpours. I joined the class a time or two, and enjoyed the peace and serenity that only "yoga on a dock-by the sea at sunrise" can bring to you...

Ak'Bol has a great snack bar right on the water where they offer an assortment of vegetarian treats and other Belizean snacks. We ran into "The Lyrical King" there. He is a local Rasta man who always has his guitar with him. He sells his recordings on the beach, and was very entertaining as he sang us several of the songs that he wrote. Imaginative, and possessing a uniquely Caribbean style, he serenaded us with his humorous lyrics. His smile was contagious, and we were drawn into his unusual music and rhythms. In a short time, we could only see the guitar on his back as he walked down the beach, with no apparent destination.

On the way back to San Pedro Town we stopped at Reef Village, a modern time-share type of resort with colorful villas on the water. It has a man-made island that you can drive your golf cart onto after crossing a tiny one-lane bridge. It is situated on the lagoon-side of the island and it has gorgeous sunsets every night of the week. Dennis Wolfe and the Usual Suspects were playing our favorite songs and it became a memorable evening for all of us.

Nothing compares to the sunset views over the lagoon, from the poolside cantina at Reef Village, while listening to a great band! SierraSky enjoyed a long swim at the pool with friends. Delightful appetizers were soon followed by another good night's sleep for all of our weary road-trippers.

The following morning our friends suggested that we take the water taxi to Caye Caulker (pronounced Key Kawker). This is one of Tina's favorite places in the world. The island is so mellow, quiet, laid-back, and a mecca for retired artists. There are no cars, only a few golf carts, and approximately one (1) truck to pick up the garbage! Everyone walks around on foot, slowly and casually. The little houses and shops are colored in beautiful pastels, Caribbean style. There are flowering trees and bushes lining the roadsides, and more butterflies than you could ever count. Belize is recognized as the butterfly and hummingbird capital of the world. Belize wins the most beautiful butterflies contest hands down!

We strolled up the island and found ourselves at The Cut which is a break between the north and south island formed by a hurricane years ago. The water flows through the deep channel from west to east, and back again with the tides.

We didn't go anywhere after that, it was too beautiful and relaxing to leave the Lazy Lizard Lounge which is situated right on the water's edge. They will rent you a snorkel, mask, and fins for $5. After swimming around and spying on the fish, you crawl out of the water exhausted and happily give them back their gear. There is so much to see underwater…a whole new world for your eyes to explore.

We loved our week with Tina and Jeff and it was memorable in many ways. I cannot recount all of the fun we had that week in a single chapter, but a fabulous time was had by all of us.

We began taking our friends, old and new, to Estelle's Restaurant on the Sea, the morning of their departure. They would ask about our tradition and it was time for honesty, "We are celebrating the fact that WE do not have to leave this beautiful island this morning. It is our way of showing how much we appreciate that we are able to remain here! Sorry…" Everyone smiled, and understood our position.

"With true friends . . . even water drunk together is sweet enough."

Chinese Proverb

Chapter 23

WORKING OUT HOW TO WORK

We discovered a website that claimed that we could start our own business in Belize right away by getting a trade license. This sounded like it would be much less complicated than getting a work permit, especially after what we had been told by our new acquaintances about the long, drawn-out process. The website we found was an individual's experience, and it listed several specific steps to follow. We assumed that we had the full story, and we started the process that it outlined: Write a letter of intent to the town board describing your business plan, get some passport photos, a police report and be sure to have the fees for filing.

We submitted a request for a local police report which came in after about thirty days. The international police report can take as long as three months to receive. It is called the Interpol report and it is a search on your identity to make sure you are not a convicted felon and are not wanted for any crimes or outstanding warrants anywhere in the world.

I wrote a letter of intent to open a nursery giving a general description of my plans. I then purchased three passport photos within minutes at a studio in town and gathered together the filing fees. Then, following the website's instructions, I submitted the whole packet to the San Pedro Town Board while crossing our fingers with the hope of receiving permission to work in Belize.

The night of the Town Board meeting, the moon happened to be full in the sign of Scorpio. We wondered how that might influence the decisions being made about our future at this special meeting. As it turned out, the meeting was called off! They re-scheduled for the following Tuesday. So we held our breath for another week.

The day of the next scheduled meeting came rather quickly and Dr. Floyd Jackson stopped by our house to give us "good news." He remembered me mentioning that I loved plants and that I was looking for some healthy seedlings. He thought that I would be happy to know that a brand new nursery just opened for business. I couldn't hide my surprise and shock! Robert and I drove down to see it right away. Sure enough, on a large lot near the sea, an extensive nursery called Ladybugs had opened on the very day of our rescheduled Town Board meeting.

The owners of the nursery must have planned things very carefully, because they did everything right. It was first-rate and it had an assortment of plants that were imported from the mainland. Our dream came true for someone else, and only a mile down the road from us. So we bought a few plants and trees, a fifty-pound sack of soil and wished them well.

We went straight to the Town Board and pulled our application within hours of that evening's board-meeting. This saved us $150 in fees. There really wasn't a need for two nurseries on our tiny island, and we didn't want to invest in a license for a business that would have some stiff competition right away. I heard that this happens often in Belize. When someone gets a good business idea, three more of them pop up around town. Everyone jumps on an idea that works. In my best recollection, not a word was said to anyone (other than close friends and family) about my plans. It's possible that my idea was borrowed after sharing with a friend who spends too much time on the coconut-telegraph. My next career plan would be kept even more confidential. "Plan B" was already mustering strength.

"What is whispered in your ear is often heard a hundred miles off."

Chinese proverb

Chapter 24

THE GREEN IGUANA ESCAPADES

Our fascination with the Green iguana started when we were living at Emerald Reef Suites. It was there that we met our first green iguana with bright red and orange stripes. He lived in the Ficus tree outside of our entrance door and we named him "Iggy." It was entertaining to go outside each morning and try to spot him because he camouflaged himself so naturally into the foliage of his green leafy home. Iguanas are experts at blending into their surroundings. Each day we would pick a fresh red hibiscus flower from the magnificent blooming bush on our porch, and place it in his tree for him to munch on. If we were not rushing off to an event that morning, we would wait patiently for him to crawl over to the flower bloom and slowly eat it. It was interesting to watch him eat the fresh flower petals and then spit out the flower bud. He was a discriminating eater who definitely knew what he liked. We also put a cup of water in the tree for him to drink.

When we moved down the beach, I went back a couple of times to see Iggy. Sadly I discovered that he was no longer there. I don't know if the neighborhood boys stole him or if he finally left on his own. He was not caged in any way, he chose to stay in that Ficus tree and enjoy the free meals that we provided.

I remember how surprised SierraSky was when she saw him for the first time. She yelled "MOM, come, come here quickly! You have to see this! MOM, Come!" Mr. Enrique, our landlord, was standing there when she found the iguana. He said "That iguana has been there for a long, long time. Please do not tell the other kids about it or they will steal him." We didn't tell her friends about him, but they may have seen us watching over him. The islanders told us that iguanas actually bond with humans when they are fed and cared for as pets, and that they have separation anxiety when their keeper leaves. I was surprised that Iggy had stayed the entire four months that we lived there. We were constantly on the porch with rowdy kids and loud guitars. To this day I wonder if Iggy left when we did or if he was taken from his tree-top home.

One afternoon, our ten-year-old neighbor "Chapu" came over with a big female iguana for sale. It was much larger than Iggy. We watched as he sold it to the man across the street for only ten Belize dollars. We asked the man if he was going to keep it as a pet, and he said "Yes." His daughter Jessica told us that they were keeping it in the bathtub. Robert observed, "That iguana is pregnant. He isn't going to keep it as a pet, because the eggs are a delicacy here in Belize. Saul is going to enjoy the eggs and then eat the iguana too." I was horrified! I found out that eating iguana is not only common in Belize but in other parts of Latin America as well. Within a week, Jessica reported that "Our cat ate the iguana when I was sleeping last night!" We still do not know for sure who ate the iguana. It wasn't talked about after the incident. We can only pray that it escaped before the dinner party began that night...

I mentioned this incident to my mom on the phone one evening. She is an animal-lover and an advocate for animal rights. She was also very disturbed by the news about the pregnant iguana. This is when my next business plan began to evolve. My mother had a suggestion that made good sense to me. "Why don't you open an iguana sanctuary?" I loved the idea! I really enjoyed watching the iguana outside our front door, and feeding it every day. Iguana's may be considered a pest and an easy meal here in Belize, but I thought that tourists who visit the island would enjoy being able to see them up-close and interact with the magnificent reptiles. I started brainstorming about making a huge cage with ficus trees and hibiscus plants in it. I pictured displaying some of the other creatures that frequent our yard as well. We have hermit crabs the size of your fist, blue land-crabs, white ghost crabs, geckos, and even a black iguana or two.

I imagined that we would decorate our front yard like a botanical garden with wonderful exotic plants and water fountains, and possibly a pair of love birds, a toucan, or maybe even a coatimundi. Tourists could wander through our yard and view the exquisite animals of the tropics. They could also relax on a bench, or in a hammock, or swing in a hammock-swing for awhile. . . This was a lovely daydream in my mind.

Robert felt differently about the whole concept. He said "No. We need more information to be successful at this." He gave me a number of valid reasons to proceed cautiously. He had done some research, as usual. He discovered that iguanas are notorious carriers of two types of salmonella, that their bodily fluids can cause a painful skin-rash, and that they are wild animals and don't do well in captivity. Furthermore, like all reptiles, they have an unpleasant odor. We also realized that we would be constantly tied to our new front-yard business, and once again, we would be giving daily care to pets.

I considered having a single green iguana as a pet instead. One afternoon "Coconut Leo" was harvesting the ripe coconuts that grow in our yard. When he came down from the tree, we found a green iguana that had been hiding in an old palm frond that dropped to the ground at our feet! The iguana was somewhat dazed. Leo was excited because he had wanted one for a pet. I knew I wasn't prepared for a pet iguana so I let him take it. I have since wondered if that was Iggy and if he had followed us to our new home just one block away. Stranger things have happened here in Belize.

Coconut Leo knew I wanted a pet iguana and he told some young local boys. They decided to go out the very next day and catch one for me. They came back with a beautiful green iguana. I was very pleased, but I explained to them that I didn't have a cage and that they needed to let it go. I was not ready to properly house my new pet. They said, "No, this iguana will live in your almond tree. It will eat the outer husk off the almonds. When they drop in the sand, you don't have to peel them. You can just crack the shell and eat the nut-meat." This sounded too good to be true.

Since Iggy lived in our ficus tree and never left, I believed the boys. They had me spit on its head and rub it in with my finger so that it would be "connected" to me. They said their uncle taught them to do that. After rubbing the spit in, we put him on the trunk of the almond tree about five feet up. Sure enough, he ran up the tree and immediately proceeded to leap off a branch into the hammock, and run across the fence out of sight! I hope you are laughing at this, because I have to laugh each time I tell this story.

I paid the boys five dollars for the iguana anyway, and hoped that it would stick around. We spotted the iguana a couple of days later, but we haven't seen him since. Robert was nonplussed when I told him what had happened and said, "Handling them can contaminate you, and they can deliver a mean bite if provoked."

My next adventure was a little more intense. The boys came back and proposed that they catch me a male and female pair. I said that sounded great, but let's wait until I am prepared with a cage. Later that week the boys returned with two beautiful iguanas. They showed me how to tell the difference between the male and female. I said "They are a gorgeous pair although I still don't have a cage." They replied "That's all right, we have one at home." So, we found a cardboard box to put the iguanas in temporarily. The boys left. A few hours later, when I thought they were never coming back, the boys limped into the yard carrying what appeared to be a very large and heavy cage. I do not know how far they carried it, but this got Robert's sympathy up and he agreed to keep the iguanas overnight, but only if I would consider releasing them in the morning.

The boys placed the cage in a central location and then tried to remove the iguanas from the box. When the iguanas saw us peering in at them, they began to race around in a terrified frenzy! They were scared, and their instincts for survival kicked in. The boys grabbed one and it was squirming around in his hands. Then the inevitable happened. He "popped" his tail! Iguanas have the ability to lose their tail if captured in order to escape. Unfortunately for him, he didn't escape after his capture, and we watched the boy stand there holding the iguana in one hand and the still moving tail in the other. I nearly fainted at the sight of his wiggling tail! The boy placed the iguana in the cage, knowing it would grow its tail back eventually.

Suddenly, we saw the tail-less iguana go running across the yard. There was a hole in the cage. It was too dark to see into the cage at this point but the boys plugged the hole with some cardboard from the box. Then they managed to successfully put the other iguana into the cage without further incident. We had experienced enough commotion for one night, so the boys were paid ten dollars for their efforts and they went home.

The next morning SierraSky was the first one out of the house and she ran over to the cage. When the iguana saw her, it started scrambling around the cage in a frenzy once again. It immediately found another hole in the cage and ran off across the yard. So far we have captured, and then quickly returned to nature, no less than three (3) iguanas!

Later that morning, when I was having my tea out on the porch, I nearly stepped on the tail-less iguana. It scared the hell out of me! I didn't expect to see it there. It had returned to the scene of the crime where the tail had been popped. Robert said "He came back hoping to find his tail." I nearly fainted again as "Mr. No-Tail" ran off once more, and I hoped he would not return anytime soon.

All of these iguana fiascos took the wind out of my reptile park idea, and Robert finally had to say, "ENOUGH, CAPTURING OF IGUANAS! They are wild creatures and need to live free." So I told the boys not to bring any more "greenies" to my house. I later found out that they are a threatened species and it is illegal to catch or cage them in Belize. So much for that brilliant plan.

"You can judge a society by the way it treats its animals."
Mahatma Gandhi

Chapter 25

UNRAVELLING THE WORK PERMIT PROCESS

We were under the impression that once we had our trade license we were approved to work. Our assumption was incorrect. In order to work in Belize, we needed to obtain a temporary work permit. The day we pulled our application for a trade license, the Town Board noticed that we didn't understand the system of obtaining a work permit in Belize, and recommended that we go speak with the Immigration and Nationalization Department.

When we inquired about the work permit application process they gave us a sheet that listed the current requirements and instructed us to gather these items and take them to the Labour Department. This was the first time we had heard of the Labour Department! Here is the list of requirements they provided:

-A photo copy of our passports

-The completed work permit application form

-Three copies of our driver's licenses

-Our police records (which were, of course, spotlessly clean!)

- Twenty dollars worth of postage stamps

-Our Belizean bank statements

-Our Trade License

-The Letter of Recommendation from the Town Board

-Our resumes (complete with degrees, certifications, diplomas, etc.)

-A Certificate of Registration for our company

We quickly realized that we were not going to get away with working with just a trade license. As we reviewed the list, we felt as though we were starting over.

"Be not afraid of growing slowly; be afraid only of standing still."
Chinese Proverb

Chapter 26

SIERRASKY LOVES SCHOOL

Another unexpected blessing! SierraSky loved school right from the start. We thought we were enrolling her in the second semester of kindergarten, but the kids here start learning their ABC's and 123's in pre-school. When they begin 1st grade at five years old, they are already putting words together and solving basic math problems. Fortunately, we had already taught SierraSky the alphabet and numbers one through ten.

Our intention was to 'home-school' SierraSky if we remained in the States. Not because of the type of curriculum offered, but because of the cultural influences in the U.S.A. Schools in Belize are heavily influenced by the British head-master system and they take the education and behavior of the students very seriously. They are strict and exacting. You are graded on your homework and on your attendance record.

We chose Isla Bonita Elementary School for her education because of its reputation for scholastic achievement. There were several schools to choose from, but I.B.E.S. just two blocks away was an obvious choice. The classrooms are small and have air-conditioning. Her class has the most members with twelve students. The school is safely placed in a peaceful neighborhood. None of the children here are "left behind." If a child doesn't understand the lesson, the teacher stays after school and will tutor them for free. The teachers in Belize are outstanding educators, and student teachers arrive from America every year as volunteers to intern with them.

SierraSky basically skipped kindergarten and started half way through first grade. At first we said to ourselves, "She is learning a whole lot more than I remember being taught in kindergarten." We began to realize that they use an advanced curriculum here and classes would be harder. She had to learn ten spelling words per week. They began reading simple books. Near the end of the semester the class was studying higher math with fractions and decimal points. She learned to count by fives and tens, and other basic addition and subtraction. In Science period they studied solids, liquids, gases, energy, matter, and astronomy.

The whole school begins each morning by singing the Belizean National Anthem in the schoolyard. It has 200 words and she knows them all by heart. English is taught as the national language, and Spanish as the secondary. She picks up "Kriol," from her friends. Kriol is the language spoken by seventy percent of Belizeans, especially the Creole people. It is similar to English and not easily understood by the un-trained ear.

We are pleased that she loves school here, and we are thrilled that she is doing well in her classes, and learning so many new things. We believe that a child's first exposure to school should be easy and fun!

SierraSky is definitely the wild-child in her school. The other school kids love her free spirit. Sometimes when I pick her up after school, I find her going around and lifting the smaller kids up with big bear hugs. They enjoyed it, but I would have to tell her,

"SierraSky, please put the little kids down, right now!" She is taller than most of her classmates and for some reason she enjoys hugging them and lifting them off their feet. They would all shriek with laughter. I would ask her teacher, "Is she well behaved? Does she listen to you, and act responsibly?" Teacher Erica would always nod "Yes" but I'd have to wonder.

In San Pedro students wear uniforms. When school lets out kids flood the streets and it is interesting to see the different schools represented by their uniforms.

If I had had to wear a uniform when I was a child I probably would have hated it. Now I appreciate them for many reasons. It is easier for the children because everyone wears the same clothes to school and there is no competition, the poor and the privileged dress alike. It is a great leveler.

SierraSky is allowed to enjoy her birthdays in class on June 12th because school doesn't let out until the end of June. Many students throw a party, complete with pizza and cake during lunch-hour.

School begins again the first of September. The tuition is $200 BZD per month which is a bargain considering the excellent education she is receiving here in Belize. The classrooms are air-conditioned to keep the students comfortable and on task.

"A child's life is like a piece of paper on which every person leaves a mark."

Chinese proverb

Chapter 27

THE RAINY SEASON BEGINS

March, April and May were warm, sunny and quite windy. Ever since the "cold spell" in January, most of our weather has been like a perfect summer day. As the sun made its way toward the equator in late March, the days got progressively hotter. Temperatures would average in the upper eighties, and by the end of May, the low nineties. It was hot with dew-points in the mid-eighties.

There was very little rain for six months. I often wondered how the lack of precipitation would affect me, but it wasn't bad at all. With lush green foliage all around it's not like a desert here. Although water rationing can be enforced during the drier months, it hasn't been necessary in recent years.

In the first week of May we had a fantastic storm with loud

thunder and lightning. Late that night a ferocious wind kicked up, and we could hear thunder in the distance. It got closer quickly, and it started pouring. The rain was welcome, but we couldn't believe the force of the wind that accompanied it! We went to the computer to see what was happening, and saw a storm the size of Belize. It was over the neighboring country, Guatemala, and it was already causing a torrential downpour on the island.

The weather centers that we checked on the computer didn't alert us to any danger. The way the house started to shimmy in the wind, we thought that this was, at the very least, in the tropical storm category. This was our first storm in Belize and they called it a tropical depression. I couldn't wait to see what an actual tropical storm would be like. This particular storm travelled on to the U.S. and devastated Nashville. My friend Tiffany, who worked at The Grand Ol' Opry, described to me what it was like to have her home, job, and city completely flooded, and under water. Mother Nature is a powerful force to reckon with.

We were happy to have made friends with the local weather specialist Mr. Winston Franklin Panton. He told us that the rainy season usually begins in June. He said the early storm was unusual for the island. The third week in May, it rained and rained and rained. We realized that we had never seen so much rain! There were even whitecaps on the sea, which we had never seen up to that point. Keep in mind, we were only in our sixth month on the island and we were still in the learning curve. More would be revealed.

We called the school at the peak of the storm that day. We asked if we should pick up the kids at lunch, or if they should just stay there and eat, because it was coming down so heavily. Most golf carts do not have windows and provide little protection from inclement weather. To our surprise the principal replied in a panicked tone "Come and get them right away, school is cancelled!" Robert put a poncho on and ventured out into the torrent through the rain-flooded muddy streets, to the little school. It was mayhem. There were taxi's lining the streets and the principal was helping the students into them and sending them home. The water was two feet deep around the schoolyard, and Robert had to carry SierraSky home on his back because the golf cart stalled in the deep water. We all wondered if it was a tropical storm building into a hurricane!

Once again, it wasn't even in the tropical storm category, and it blew over later that afternoon. When the final tally was in, it was determined that the island received 10.86 inches of rain on May 19th, the all time record on Ambergris Caye! We suspected that it was an unusual amount of rain. It also broke the record for highest rainfall in an hour, totaling 6 inches between noon and 1 pm. That sort of cloudburst is unimaginable in Wisconsin.

The rainy season is also called the "green season" because of the renewal that takes place on the Caye after a good soaking. Everything gets a drink. Plants revive and bloom. The sea salt and sand are rinsed away by the rain to expose the lush green of the palm trees, the almond trees, the bougainvilleas, and the banana trees. Empty cisterns refill. Hundreds of giant puddles form in the street. The raincoats, umbrellas and ponchos come out of the closet for the season, and the Belizeans go back to work, business as usual. I must confess here, that the mosquitoes that disappeared for 6 months, returned to paradise...hungry!

"Barometer, n.: An ingenious instrument which indicates what kind of weather we are having."

Ambrose Bierce, *The Devil's Dictionary*

"Don't knock the weather. If it didn't change once in a while, nine out of ten people couldn't start a conversation."

Kin Hubbard

Chapter 28

GATHERING OUR WORK PERMIT REQUIREMENTS

We started out in Belize hugely optimistic about choosing a career here, and going into business somewhere on the island. When we were given the list of items needed for the work permit application from Immigration we were somewhat overwhelmed, a bit daunted, but not discouraged. Some of the items on the list were simple and easy to acquire. We already had the photo copies of our passports, three copies of our driver's licenses and our police reports which had finally come in. We purchased twenty dollars worth of postage stamps and we completed the lengthy, and sometimes confusing, work permit application form.

Unfortunately, we were totally lost when it came to the Certificate of Registration for our company. We needed to form a company. We discovered that if you are not a resident and you want to be a business owner, you have to have a Belizean partner in the company. We had developed a trusted friendship with a local Belizean and she was willing to sign as a partner.

To form a company you can either file for a company registrar for $150 at the Town Board or you can form a corporation. We learned that we could employ the services of an offshore bank to develop a corporation which cost approximately $2500. A hefty stack of paperwork is developed governing your business profile, and there are lots of signature lines at the end. After a filing fee and a two-month wait, we finally had our business registered and created. We chose to name it "Bare-Toes."

Getting a Belizean bank account was not so easy. We had been informed early on by our ex-pat friends that it is smart to get a Belizean bank account established. They had mentioned that if you can show via monthly bank statements that income is flowing into the country, it would come in handy some day during the work-permit and residency applications process. With that advice we looked into acquiring bank accounts right away when we arrived.

Establishing a bank account was easier for me than it was for Robert. We had decided to sell the pet food business that was in my name in the States, and therefore the income from the sale was in my name. You must explain the source of any assets over $10,000 dollars, and allow your U.S. banking records to be seen by the local banks. I contacted the Belize International Bank prior to our move to the island. I was told that I secured my off-shore bank account in the nick of time, because the laws that the U.S. were imposing internationally were about to become much more strict. I was relieved to have my account opened before things became even more complicated.

After showing the International Belize Bank the purchase agreement for the sale of our business, and providing them with two bank references from the States, they set me up with a savings account with an attractive interest rate. They also helped me set up a savings account with the Belize Bank that earned 6% BZD. They were happy to have my money, and were very polite and respectful to me.

Robert on the other hand had a more difficult experience with opening a bank account. He had an excellent banking history, and A-1 credit in the United States. He had to solicit two letters of recommendation from two different banks, and they had to be written and notarized by his Wisconsin bankers. They also required him to provide his U.S. banking statements to be examined. It took three weeks to open an account.

Our resumes, complete with certificates, diplomas, etc., were easy enough to write. Since Robert and I were self-employed for most of our lives, we had never needed to create a resume before. The process of reflection over all of the trades and trials and tribulations that we had been through over the years was interesting, amusing, and a bit mind-blowing when we realized that all of our hard work led us to our warm, tropical paradise.

During all the preparation for the work permit application, it became abundantly clear that getting our permits, and starting new careers, is actually a long, and sometimes frustrating journey. Robert kept saying, "If it was easy, everyone would live here and they would all be your next-door neighbors!"

"Man who waits for roast duck to fly into mouth must wait very, very long time."

Chinese proverb

Chapter 29

SUZANNE SINGS BELIZE

Godmother Suzanne came to visit for SierraSky's birthday the first and second weeks of June to see what Belize was all about. She knew how much we missed her and she dutifully saved her pennies until she could afford to visit us in our new island home.

Suzanne is a blast! So full of life, and always looking for fun things to do! Her visit was a breath of fresh air for SierraSky. She knew what was in store for her. Suzy will do art projects, swim every day, walk all the beaches on the island, and play with her until she finally collapses from exhaustion.

Once again we were able to share this beautiful island and show it off to our friend from Wisconsin. Suzanne enjoys many of the same interests that we have, and this was sure to lead to an especially good time for all of us.

SierraSky ran to the front gate as soon as she saw her Godmother coming across the sand, and gave her a great big hug. She was excited to see her again, and her eyes got big like saucers. It was a heartwarming moment. They love each other and share many happy memories.

The fun began immediately as Suzie started handing out presents! SierraSky's friends were there, and were thrilled as Suzanne dug through her bag and doled out squirt guns, stickers, little mini kites and all the things that kids love. They ran off to the dock as soon as they could, to fly their little sparkly butterfly kites. We could hear the giggling and laughter from our front porch. Of course they had their kites all tangled together and crashed in the sea within fifteen minutes.

I was thrilled that Suzanne loves to swim like I do. Not everyone is up for going swimming every day. The kids enjoy it, but that tends to be more like babysitting than a day at the beach. SierraSky was still in school for Suzanne's first few days here so Suzie and I went swimming without the kids a few times. We inflated the rafts, grabbed our goggles, snorkels and fins, slapped on the sun-block and headed to the end of the long boat dock near our casita. She discovered the same things that I did when I took my first swim in the Caribbean Sea. The water is extremely clear and warm! Due to the high salt content, you are quite buoyant. I told her that you float easily without even trying, and we do not actually need rafts, but she discovered this on her own. You need a weight-belt to swim to the bottom!

We secured our goggles and dove under the water to find the peaceful colorful world that lies below the surface. It is hard to stop watching the blue tangs, the yellow snappers, the white grunts, and those long-nosed needle-fish. There are black and yellow striped fish called seargent majors that SierraSky named "Nemo fish," and a multitude of other colorful sea creatures under the pier. What I find most adorable, are the baby fish; itty-bitty Nemo's swimming around, and teeny-weeny newborn sardines if you can imagine how precious they are! Eventually, you have to lift your head up for air and return to the whispers of the sea breezes in your ears, the roaring sound of the waves breaking on the reef, and the buzz of an occasional motor boat passing by. It's back to the real world above the waterline.

Suzanne has a life-long fascination with sting rays, also referred to as "skates" and "rays." She bought a beautiful hand sculpted wooden stingray from a street vendor for a good price. She certainly came to the right place for skate-watchin'. She was so excited the first time she saw a fisherman cleaning his catch and the cluster of rays that gathered in the water at his feet. It was captivating to see the sting-rays feeding on the discarded fish scraps, their long tails thrashing as they competed for a free meal.

Suzanne also reveres sea turtles. When we chartered Mr. Mercedes glass-bottom boat to swim at the reserve, she was lucky enough to witness the largest sea turtle she has ever seen. We must have been in the right place at the right time because we were blessed with the chance sighting of three baby turtles. They were enchanting. As usual, there were nurse sharks, jack mackerel and huge stingrays at the park that afternoon. Suzanne showed her courage by riding home on the roof of the boat with me. What a trooper! (She wouldn't swim with the sharks though :)

Suzie happened to arrive on one of the hottest days of the year. The heat index was 110 degrees! We had to keep our "dew-rags" close by while we sat on the front porch and sang old favorites, constantly wiping our brows. The dew point and humidity were so high that water would just condense on your skin. The sunshine hits the water and sends water vapor into the air surrounding the island. Thankfully, there is usually a nice breeze from the sea and at dusk everything begins to cool off and the evening fun begins!

Suzanne is in a band. A born torch-singer, she has always loved music and musicians. It has been her hobby and favorite pastime for many years. In the States she has been known to win a karaoke contest or two, (1st place in Northern Illinois!) and various other singing contests. We introduced her to our favorite band, and they loved her vocal style. She really knocked them out at the many Karaoke bars around San Pedro. She made us proud. What a songbird Suzanne has become. It was very amusing to watch the locals follow her act. She was good enough to make them nervous.

We saw people at karaoke that we know from various businesses around town and watched them get up and sing, looking to Suzanne for approval! We also saw the immigration officer sing

Sinatra's "I Did It My Way," and let me tell you, he sure did! He has since been transferred.

I don't know if it was her love for us, the swimming, the singing, or the fresh fruit and sunshine, but something made Suzie decide to extend her stay. She changed her flight schedule for her return trip home, and soaked up a little more Belizean sunshine and love, before returning to "life as usual" back in the States. It was great having her visit us, and we anxiously await her encore performance here on La Isla Bonita.

"When the character of a man is not clear to you, look at his friends.

Japanese Proverb

Chapter 30

THE BIRTHDAYS

June has always been a big birthday celebration month in our family. Grandpa John's birthday is on June 11th, SierraSky's on the 12th, Aunt Cindi's is the 13th and God-mother Suzanne's birthday is on the 15th. Our new friends Joy and Frank have birthdays that begin and end the month of June.

We had a party on the 11th with SierraSky's classmates at school. They all sang happy birthday Belizean-style and we served a beautiful purple cake that SierraSky picked out. Then she opened presents from her classmates. One of her friends, Rhea, brought her a Barbie-doll set that must have cost $200!

That weekend, SierraSky had a party at the Fitness Center with her four closest friends. They had fun swimming and jumping off the bridge into the deep water of the Olympic sized pool.

After we wore out the kids we headed back to our house for a slumber party. We played the typical party games; musical chairs, pin-the-tail on the crocodile, red light, green light, and busted-open the homemade piñata! SierraSky was blindfolded and shattered it to pieces with one mighty blow. Her friends were like hungry piranhas scooping up all the candy before she could even remove her blindfold. She began to cry and her friends quickly gave her ALL of their candy to make her happy again. It was sweet to see that moment. Soon, we were eating fresh pan-fried black snapper that Robert prepared perfectly, with Belizean mashed potatoes. It was heavenly. We sang Happy Birthday at least three times. Then it was time for us to eat her delicious homemade, hand-decorated cake with ice cream! She said it was her "Best birthday ever!"

With the festivities slowing down a bit, we were hoping to tuck the girls into bed at a reasonable hour. Much to our dismay, we began to hear music and discovered that there was a graduation party next door. The neighbors are Mexican- Belizeans and they have huge family parties. We knew we were in for a late night when everyone and their cousin started arriving for this grand event at around 9pm. A festive band named Rompe Raja started to play around 9:30. It had to be the loudest band I have ever heard!I realized there wouldn't be any sleeping, any time soon. Belizean parties are notorious for starting late and ending at dawn.

The movie the girls were watching was over at 11:00 pm, and five very awake kids asked me what was next. We had served them a late night snack hoping that it would help make them sleepy, and I told them a few bed-time stories. Meanwhile, the neighbor's party got louder and louder. More and more people were arriving. I hoped that the party would end at midnight but no such luck. My patience was wearing thin. I told the kids, lights-out and I don't want to hear another peep. At mid-night the band finally stopped, and we cheered! A few minutes later, after an obvious tequila break, Rompe Raja started playing again. On and on they played until 2:30 am. Somehow the kids fell asleep by 1:00 am.

On July 4th the neighbors directly behind us, threw a 7th birthday-bash for SierraSky's friend, Marbella. It was a semi-formal affair with all the little girls in their finest dresses. The mommies dressed up as well. Everyone looked so elegant in their Sunday best! They had a DJ blasting punta music all evening and decorations galore. The children played all the standard party games for two hours, and SierraSky won "stop-dance" twice. Her prizes were extravagant. They spare no expense at these family affairs!

At these parties, the food had better be delicious, plentiful, and served hot, or else! This is how the Belizeans report their current status to relatives and close friends. I am happy to report that the food was fantastic! Soon after the party began, excellent appetizers were served, one after another. That night, there must have been seven courses brought out into the yard from the hacienda kitchen, and served with refreshments. On the food list was: lobster cheese dip, ever-flowing beer and rum punch, Belizean chicken wings, Mexican mashed potatoes, sliced smoked ham, more beer and punch, three types of potato salads, fried chicken, more beer and punch, finger sandwiches, and an assortment of appetizers that we had never seen before! They also served a full turkey dinner with all the side dishes. The elder family members are served first, out of respect. Turkey is considered to be an expensive delicacy in these parts, and is seen as a status symbol because of its price and availability!

We were astounded at the effort put forth for a 7-year-old's birthday party. They have an even bigger event when a Belizean girl turns fifteen. It is called Quince-Anos, and is a rite of passage into womanhood. They are the biggest parties on the island; more opulent and costly than a wedding. Families have been known to mortgage their houses to stage this event! We can't wait to attend one. We are currently trying to make friends with a family that has a 14 year old daughter. Just kidding!

My birthday is July 12th and has been overshadowed a bit since SierraSky was born. It was nice to be recognized again. Robert & friends chartered a full day on the Lady Leslie, a 50 foot catamaran. We sailed to Caye Caulker to spend the day at The Cut. It was a beautiful day with sunny blue skies and white puffy clouds. I enjoyed my best snorkeling experience ever at Hol Chan on the way to our neighboring island. After a two hour swim, we continued to our destination. They were celebrating Lobster-fest that day in Caye Caulker, and there were dozens of imaginative lobster meals available to choose from! We enjoyed lobster lunch and snacks for a couple of hours before returning to the boat. We were sated with delicious seafood.

As we headed back to the catamaran, an immense purple raincloud began to cover the island. The tropical rains and wind exploded right away! Running to the sailboat in the downpour was our only option. Captain Martin was anxious to leave before the next storm arrived. Back in the safety of our sturdy craft, we all huddled in the cabin as we waited for the storm to blow over. When there was a break in the storm we headed out to sea. It was the most exciting boat ride I've ever had. Thunder rolled and echoed all around us. When the rain hit again, we all sat under the canopy and enjoyed the moment as raindrops splashed all around us. Before returning to San Pedro Town my ship-mates sang "Happy Birthday to Lydia" and, for the sixth time in six weeks, everybody ate cake.

The next morning we woke up to discover our golf cart missing! We left the catamaran with our hands full the night before. It was dark out and still pouring rain. We hustled into our casita exhausted and soaked. Neither of us remembered to lock the cart. We knew this might happen eventually. If you forget to lock your cart at night, it can be taken for a joy ride by someone who has had too much to drink and doesn't feel like walking all the way home. ALL golf-cart keys fit ALL golf-carts! The thieves usually leave the "borrowed" cart near their house and walk the rest of the way home so no one can connect them to the crime.

We reported that our cart was stolen to the police, the Taxi Driver Association and our friends in hopes that someone would spot it. Soon, the coconut telegraph was buzzing with the offer of a small reward. We called Polo's rental and rented a cart to facilitate our search. We hunted for our cart from one end of the island to the other. Unfortunately, our rental cart was an electric one and the batteries died miles up north in the middle of nowhere. I found myself running alongside the cart to lessen the strain on the batteries. Robert was laughing hysterically as I tried in vain to push the cart back to civilization.

We were overjoyed when we got the call from Polo. He informed us that someone who had spotted our stolen cart had called and offered to tell us where it was... for a nominal fee. Polo picked us up where we were stranded. He found us "toughing it out" at the Palapa Bar, one of the island's best watering-holes. We paid the $100 BZD reward and Polo gave us a ride to our 'lost' cart. We were never so happy to see it! It was four miles south in a huge mud puddle. It wouldn't start and they left it there for us to eventually find.

That night we went out to hear some live music, dance under the stars, and eat more cake with our new local compadres. Everyone had a great time, especially me! It was, without a doubt, a birthday that we will never forget..."A diplomat is a man who always remembers a woman's birthday but never remembers her age." Anonymous

Chapter 31

OUR CAREER WAS DECIDED FOR US

Robert and I mulled over dozens of ideas about what we should do for income here on the island. We agreed that time spent earning a living uses up a significant portion of our lives and that choosing a career should be a well thought-out decision. This time around we were trying to pick a career that was not stressful and demanding. We weren't looking to get rich. We wanted to be happy.

Most importantly we agreed that we wanted to earn a living without creating another rush-rush, rat-race, high-tension, blood-pressure raising, super-competitive, physically-and-mentally-exhausting situation like the one we left behind in America.

I considered the possibility of studying herbal medicine with a renowned "bush-doctor" to learn about Mayan health remedies. That idea still holds my interest but I would have to spend too much time away from my family. This is a field that would have to become a way of life for me, with several years of experience under my belt before I would be able to practice herbal medicine in Belize. I decided to put that idea on hold. What is life without our dreams...?

I wanted to put up a hammock park in our front yard, but after some serious reflection on the nursery idea, and the iguana sanctuary plan, Robert realized that he didn't want a bunch of people hanging out on our property all day long and into the night. This would be another serious invasion of privacy! We did the "business-across the-street thing" for a number of years in Wisconsin. It has its positive points, as well as its challenges. We try not to repeat our mistakes.

We toyed around with the idea of having a bar or restaurant. It could be fun, but WAY too much work, pressure, and stress. There were several opportunities to manage bars on the island and Robert had decades of experience in the food and beverage industry. We reminded ourselves that we came to Belize to live a more laid-back lifestyle, and we chose to put the bar-restaurant management idea on hold as well.

We could have debated, dreamed, and pondered our career choices forever but there was something we didn't know. After talking more with the officials about working here, we were informed that it didn't matter what we *wanted* to do here, but rather what we were *approved* to do. The Labour Department, Immigration Department, the Town Board, and various other "powers that be" wanted to see proof that we had professional skills. They required certificates, documents, diplomas, and our list of qualifications in our application for a work permit. They carefully screen immigrants to make sure that we are going to offer something helpful to the community. You cannot get a work-permit for a job that Belizeans are qualified for. Specialized professionals like architects, engineers, hotel managers, doctors, etc. can easily attain a work-permit. The government DOES NOT welcome indigent beach-bums!

If we were buying property or purchasing a restaurant that employed San Pedranos, it would be easier to get our work permits and residency status. They welcome the wealthy, potential investors, people who purchase property on the island, or who invest in a local business.

We looked over our credentials and decided which career path we would have to take based on our skills that we had documents to substantiate.

"To open a shop is easy, to keep it open is an art." Chinese proverb

Chapter 32

SEPTEMBER

We heard that San Pedro Town "shuts down" for the month of September. At that time of the year the tourist season is very slow and many hotels and restaurants close for the whole month. The islanders who work in the tourist industry take a break to go on vacation or to visit their families on the mainland. Many of the hotel workers leave their jobs, which are waiting for them when they return.

When we were told that the high season slows down after Easter we were surprised at how many tourists were still in town. To us, it appeared to be a steady stream of visitors. We wondered just how quiet September actually got. They were right! It is an extremely slow month for tourism. Very few gringos vacation here in September. Kids are going back to school and preparations for fall and winter are in full force. The ex-patriots and other locals are the only ones left to keep the few open stores up and running.

During this time, two of our good friends had to leave the island behind. Our dear friend Bob, who was Robert's guitar pickin' buddy lost his job. He sold high-end timeshares and condos, and the condo colony closed. After 5 ½ years of steady sales on the island, his job just fizzled out. Back to Colorado he went. We will miss him every day until we meet again.

We will also miss our Canadian friend Nicole. Her bar and restaurant closed in June, and she came by to announce her move to Placencia, a coastal village in southern Belize where the prices are quite a bit cheaper. The island will never be the same without her happy, gregarious and fun-loving personality.

During the slow season I found that I had more free time on my hands and Mrs. Dennis Wolfe, "Dulce" invited me to join the local ladies bridge group. It was a privilege to be asked to join because it was a tight-knit qroup of women. Most of the players had been raised on the island or had lived here for decades and had earned status and prestige in the community. I was the new kid on the block and I didn't know how to play bridge! Choosing to decline the invitation could have been social-suicide, so I asked Dulce to teach me the game.

The ladies were competitive about cards and one in particular was disgruntled that I wasn't skilled in playing bridge yet. My friend Emma was also in the group. Noticing my discomfort she suggested that I switch to another weekly card game called "Oh Hell!" The women in that group were also established ladies of Ambergris Caye, and I was delighted to find myself in a club that was fun and laid back.

The women in this group were an eclectic mix of well-educated artists, retired business women, proprietors, authors, property owners, and housewives. Most of them moved here from the States and Canada and have been living here for many, many years. They took me under their wings. I quickly learned that finger food and local gossip were very important parts of these gatherings. Playing cards was just an excuse to get together to laugh, talk about news on the island, and discuss where the good deals on groceries and other necessities were to be found in San Pedro. Each week was always an entertaining and educating experience.

Although September is one of the quietest months for tourism, it is a month full of wild and vibrant celebrations for the Belizeans. Saint George's Caye Day get's the party started with its week-long festival from September 3rd through the 10th.

There are parades throughout the month. We would be sitting on our upper porch in the middle of the day and suddenly a parade would pass by! One of the big events is the Children's Parade and it is filled with enthusiastic kids and lots of candy. All ten of the primary schools march their students down the street. There are over 2,000 students enrolled in the public school alone. They are adorable in their uniforms and very proud of their school identities. We knew the population of children on Ambergris Caye was incredibly large, but we had never seen them all in one place until the Children's Parade. It was fun to see them march to the drummers. Everyone waves to the onlookers, and they flash them wide, happy smiles.

Independence Day falls on September 21st. In America, Independence Day is sort of a mythical holiday, based on events that transpired over 200 years ago. The newly independent Belizeans are extremely patriotic! It has only been a few decades since they got their independence, and a brand-new constitution was put into effect. Many of the people who made it happen are still alive. They worked very hard to create Belizean sovereignty from British rule, and they are quite proud of it! Everyone decorates their carts and businesses with the Belizean national flag, and the streets are full of the red, white, blue, and green waving banners flapping in the breeze.

There are carnivals, talent shows and concerts. On the eve of Independence Day, they blow off fireworks at midnight, and drummer boys parade the streets. The party goes on ALL night long.

The Independence Day parade was the best. We were supposed to march in it with SierraSky's class, but the streets were overflowing with people, and we couldn't get to where the parade was starting. We were content watching from a shady spot instead of walking for miles in the hot noon-day sun. I was actually relieved that I didn't have to march when I saw that the school participants were wearing white t-shirts and that all the women were soaked from unexpected cloudbursts during the parade.

It was unlike any parade I had ever seen. Participants were dancing behind brightly decorated floats with giant speakers piping out loud music from the local DJ's private collections. People were dressed in their costumes of various themes. Spirit, pride, and enthusiasm poured out of the marching groups. Music blasted through the biggest P.A. systems we had ever seen! When the thunderstorm rolled through, rain was pouring down and everyone was soaked. They didn't mind a bit. It seemed like they enjoyed it even more as the rain cooled off the crowd and the streets. The sun returned and quickly dried everyone off as they continued the festive celebration.

When I think of Independence Day in the States, it reminds me of barbecue cook-outs with friends. Usually there was a lame and boring parade which was always too early in the morning and fireworks with too many mosquitoes at night. Our traditional 4th of July holiday somehow lacks meaning nowadays, and it doesn't honor the original ideals that it purported. It appears that we may have lost some of our enthusiasm, when we celebrate the signing of the most important document in our country's history, The Declaration of Independence, and the creation of the American

Constitution including the Bill of Rights.

When this little town celebrates, it parties down! In the parade the floats have water and juices for the kids and five gallon jugs of rum punch and "coco-loco" for the adults. Belikin drives their company truck on the parade route, and they hand out one thousand bottles of icy cold beer to all the thirsty bystanders, free of charge. The people in the parade get drunk and silly and pour drinks for the spectators, and the spectators hand drinks back to them. The policemen, firemen, bankers, teachers, shop owners, and politicians drink and dance together in the street. If this parade were in the States, everyone involved would be arrested. Drinking, driving, and dancing in the streets? The cops in America would throw a net over us all. This is a no-holds-barred, pure celebration of life independence!

If you ever visit San Pedro Town, make sure you come on September 21st for an event you will never forget. They love their independence in Belize!

"A wise man makes his own decisions, an ignorant man follows the public opinion." Chinese proverb

Chapter 33

LETTER OF RECOMMENDATION TAKES ITS SWEET TIME

Robert and I were disappointed that we had to request the type of job that we were already experienced in and qualified for. We had hoped to try something fresh and new that we hadn't done before. When a new piece of information came to us from the ex-patriots, we were excited! We were told that if you are approved as a "business owner," you are basically entitled to do any type of work pertaining to it.

Robert chose to pursue music and wanted to perform again. After playing in a band for over half of his life, co-managing a music store for 10 years, and selling high end guitars for the last 15 years, music had always put bread on his table. We were told by the Ex-pat's, and other island workers, that they would not let him apply as a working musician because it would take a potential job from a Belizean. So we decided to go through a side door by applying as a business owner who provides music lessons, equipment rentals, and band management.

In an effort to receive a letter of recommendation, and a trade license from the Town Board, Robert wrote a letter of intent stating that he would like to offer his skills by teaching guitar, piano, drums, (and pretty much any instrument you can think of) as well as doing band management, performance, and recitals.

As for me, I wrote a letter of intent requesting to offer my services as a pet-nutrition counselor, and pet-sitter in the community. I didn't really want to continue in the canine-care department, but it looked like I would have to go back into that field of work, or at least claim to be. There are many people here who cherish their dogs as much as their own children, and take excellent care of them. These would be my new customers.

I mentioned that I would give nutritional advice In my letter of intent and the Town Board informed me that I would have to get an approval from the top veterinarian in Belize. When I called his clinic they referred me to the Chairman of the Board of Veterinarians. I was impressed! I didn't know Belize had one.

The man I was referred to was very kind and willing to help. He told me that he would put something in writing for free. When I received his letter of approval I took it back to the Town Board and hoped they would issue me a letter of recommendation and trade license.

I wish we had known about the letter of recommendation from the Town Board sooner. I was told that it would only take a few days to get the letter and surprisingly there was no fee for this step, but it took more than six weeks. My tenacity finally paid off, but looking back, paying someone may have expedited the process after all.

It requires a lot of patience to deal with the Town Board, Immigration, and all the different regulations and requirements to open a new business here. This is a country where patience is taught on a daily basis. "Belize Time" is quite a bit different than what we were used to. Be prepared to wait for what you want. It will come in time.

Belize is still getting a foot in the twenty-first century. Almost every official document is hand written in triplicate, with the use of carbon-paper. In many offices, they do not use computers to store files. It's done the old-fashioned way. Stacks of folios in every corner of the room, not a filing cabinet in sight! We were told time and again to be sure to make copies of any official papers that you turn in because they may accidentally misplace it. Then you must start the whole process of filing your written requests from the beginning. This is common knowledge in Belize.☺

September was a month full of celebrations. Between the holidays and hurricane threats, the Town Board was frequently closed. I am sure they were kept very busy planning all of the holiday events. There is always much more that goes into planning a celebration than meets the eye. We have learned to slow down, and enjoy life! It will all get done. My new favorite Belizean saying is: "I think I will save a little work for tomorrow!" The Belizeans like to stay busy, and since they know there probably won't be a blizzard anytime soon, they have the luxury of taking their time to finish a project.

The following account is a typical example of how things get done in Belize:

The assistant to the mayor received our request for the Letter of Recommendation and gave it to her assistant to review. When I thought the letter would be ready, I stopped back in and the assistant's assistant wasn't in that day. The next week I stopped in and asked about the paperwork, and was told that the mayor had it on her desk to review but she was on the mainland for a few days. When I stopped in the *next* week and questioned the assistant, she informed me that the mayor had "not gotten to it" yet. I told her that I understood that she must have very important matters to handle. She kindly replied that all matters were important, including ours, and that "she would be sure to call us when the letters were ready" as she wrote down our phone number.

After giving it *another* week, I stopped in at the Town Board again. I didn't want to appear to be a pestering, impatient gringo but I thought that the mayor must have the letter signed by now.

When I saw the assistant she smiled and handed me the envelope with our letters of recommendation inside! I didn't ask why she didn't call me, I was just glad to finally have it in my hands. That was on the 23rd of the month. The letter was signed and dated on the 12th! I love Belize, and I have learned to appreciate what I get. Good things take time...

Eventually we procured our trade license as well. We were unaware that you cannot have a trade license unless you are a resident and if you aren't one, you need a Belize citizen to be on the trade license with you. Fortunately, our close friend was willing to sign on the trade license with us.

We began the trade license application process in May and then cancelled it because someone beat us to the chase on the nursery idea. In July we were approved for our new trade license with the plan of Robert teaching music and me being a pet sitter. We didn't actually receive our trade licenses from the town board until late August. All trade licenses are renewed on Jan. 1'st, so we were only charged for a half year, the fee being $150BZ. I thought that Robert and I would be on one trade license but I was approved for a trade license of my own and was expected to buy it. (Belize rhymes with fees!)

At last, we finally had our letter of recommendations and trade licenses which completed our list of things to gather in order to apply for our work permit. Wow! That took a while...

"Patience is a tree with bitter roots that bears sweet fruits."

Chinese proverb

Chapter 34

WORKING ON WORKING WITH THE LABOUR DEPARTMENT

We finally went in to the Labor Department on Tuesday, October 19th, brimming with curiosity about what the experience was going to be like! With our packets in hand we headed up the stairs. The secretary politely told us that they only review work permit applications on Wednesdays. Conveniently, that was the next day and we weren't too disappointed with one more delay. We left with our curiosity, and our paperwork, to wait some more.

The next day we sat nervously in the lobby of the Labour Department again, wondering what to expect. After a lengthy wait we were introduced to the man in charge of work permits, Mr. George. He was extremely kind and friendly. It was a relief to find him helpful and receptive to our plan of action. Unfortunately, he told us that the list of requirements that we had was out-dated, and that there were a few more details that we needed to complete our applications:

-A $25 dollar administration fee receipt for each of us (more fees!)

- three recent passport size photos instead of the drivers license photo-copies

-copies of ALL of the pages of our passports, even the blank ones, to prove we paid for our monthly stamps since we had arrived in Belize

- And last, but not least, we needed back-up documentation and preferably certificates and diplomas to prove that we were qualified to perform the work and trade skills that we claimed to have.

We scrambled around town getting the new items that we needed. We thought we would gather some extra proof from locals to help us along.

To confirm that Robert is a talented musician, we attained a letter from SierraSky's principal that stated that Robert had indeed joined the school in many outings such as the campfire on the beach, Christmas caroling, and leading the kids in song at her school with his guitar. The letter also stated that they would be pleased if Robert would teach students from Isla Bonita Elementary School. We also printed photos of Robert playing an assortment of instruments with various people on our porch, including the principal's nephew whom he was unofficially teaching as a gesture of goodwill.

I included my letter from the Chairman of the Board of Veterinarians, who gave me approval to pet sit and give nutritional advice. I also provided ample brochures and flyers from our business, The Dog Spot of Lake Geneva.

We finally took our applications in on Friday October 29th, because Mr. George said that he would be happy to meet with us on a day other than Wednesday, if need be. That day happened to be the afternoon before Halloween week-end, which of course was another big opportunity to celebrate here in San Pedro Town.

Mr. George was once again very kind. He glanced through the stacks of documents briefly and confirmed that at last we had completed all of the forms and necessary requirements! We couldn't have been more surprised when he handed them back to us. We said "Don't you need to keep them?" He said "No, you keep the packets. When I have more time next week, come back and I will go over them with you more thoroughly and sign off on them." "Ohhh-Kaaaay" we replied. We put on our best smiles and said, "We'll see you next week! Have a spooky Halloween!"

The following week we went in on Wednesday, and Mr. George reviewed our applications in detail. He told us that he was in approval of our requests. This news brought great joy to our hearts but we sensed there was a catch. He informed us that he now signs off on them and sends the work permit application packets to Belmopan for the Labour Board committee to approve, and that we should hear back from them in three to four weeks!

After three weeks we went back to see Mr. George. We were sorry to hear that he had not received any news yet, but he said this is a good sign because if something was questionable, they would have contacted him and requested more information. He suggested that we check back in a couple of weeks. With all of the time, effort, preparation, help from our friends, and running around, we hoped that our work-permits were just around the corner.

"Pick the flower when it is ready to be picked" Chinese Proverb

Chapter 35

PARADISE FOR SALE!

This was a jagged little pill to swallow.

When we went to our landlord with the intention of pre-paying our lease, I received some disturbing news that I never expected. Someone had just made an offer to buy the beach-house that we were renting. It wasn't listed for sale and the landlord hadn't planned on selling it. Money talks and times are tough here on the Island. Our landlord was caught in the construction crunch and needed some cash to help his business survive.

One afternoon we saw a couple of tourists staring at our house from the beach. Apparently, they tracked down the owner and made him an offer he couldn't refuse! The offer was $500,000. USD. They liked the area, and decided on the spot that they wanted the house. Robert said that it's worth half of that amount and it probably wouldn't sell anytime soon, especially with the banks tightening up on loans.

Are you familiar with the expression "They yanked my security blanket" Or "It felt like the carpet was pulled out from underneath me"? In this case, it may have been a magic carpet ride. . .

I learned at least three life lessons right away:

Non-attachment. Do not embrace material things. I had fallen into an emotional trap! I was so excited about living in our beautiful house on the sea, that I found myself taking pride in it. I freely spoke of where we lived to anyone that asked. I was soon humbled by my false-pride. Slowly, after a day or two of getting used to the idea, I started letting go of this attachment.

See the beauty in everything. When I realized that we were going to have to move sooner than I had ever dreamed of, I was confused. I thought, where do we go when we have already had the best? The rest of the island seemed less beautiful than where we had been living. I didn't want to consider renting any house or apartment after comparing it to our beachfront abode. I reminded myself that I had to see the beauty in all things.

Gratitude. Don't just thank God when being given something grand. One has to have faith that things are working out for the best, no matter what happens, or how bad it may seem. It's easy to be thankful and count your lucky stars when you get something you want. It's also easy to get mad at God, or the universe, when something is taken away. It is a challenge to be thankful, and truly grateful each day, especially when things don't go the way we expect them to. It requires great faith to know that "the universe is unfolding exactly as it should" when we are in a situation that we would not have chosen for ourselves.

It's a good thing I didn't set up a business in the front yard. I would have wasted a lot of money! I am glad that I had a couple of other ideas brewing. Maybe this change prevented that particular path from unfolding, in order to steer us onto a path that is more aligned with our ideals. Jerry Jeff Walker once said: "Anything that ain't a mystery is simply guesswork!" I tend to agree with him.

We were in limbo. We didn't know if the American couple was going to return and actually buy the house. We wondered if the landlord was hoping that we would buy it. He did tell us we could make him an offer. We were in no position to buy a house at the time, so we just decided to enjoy this slice of heaven while we had it, and start looking with an open mind at the other possibilities on the island. We hoped we would find a place that we would enjoy even more than La Casita.

In John Lennon's own words, "Life is what happens to you, while you're busy making other plans."

Thanks to this little 'twist' in our path, our resolve was strengthened. We forged ahead, resolving to enjoy every day that we had left in our beach cottage. I recalled the book by Dr. Richard Alpert, (aka Baba Ram Dass) entitled "Be Here Now" which reminds us to "live in the moment!" We looked forward to the next surprise in our lives! Sometimes things turn out much better than we anticipate. Only time would tell. This chinese proverb is said when bad luck turns to good, or when good luck turns to bad

"Sāi Wēng lived on the border and he raised horses for a living. One day he lost a horse and his neighbor felt sorry for him, but Sāi Wēng didn't care about the horse, because he thought it wasn't a bad thing to lose a horse. After a while the horse returned with another beautiful horse, and the neighbor congratulated him on his good luck. But Sāi Wēng thought that maybe it wasn't a good thing to have this new horse."

"His son liked the new horse a lot and often took it riding. One day his son fell off the horse and broke his leg. Because of his broken leg, he couldn't go off to the war, as was expected of all the young men in the area. Most of them died.".

Chapter 36

BEACH DOGS

At the Dog Spot of Lake Geneva, we were surrounded by dogs that had it made! The owners came in to buy the best types of food, and have their dogs groomed. Some clients washed their own dogs in the do-it-yourself dog-wash. Dogs came every day to play with other dogs in our day care facility. Their owners were pleased that their dogs weren't stuck at home alone, lethargic, and bored. People carefully chose our facility to board their dogs when they were out of town, knowing that they would receive the best overnight care for their pets.

Most of the dogs we encountered were all meticulously cared for. They were well fed and often fed a little too much. They were brought to training class to correct behavioral problems, and some of them learned to be better pets. Numerous dogs were loved so much that their owners showed it by letting them rule the roost, and even allowed them to sleep on their beds. Yes, some of the dogs were just plain spoiled rotten!

We had heard about the dogs in Central and South America; how they ran wild in the streets and were under-fed and malnourished. We imagined that they were starving, begging, flea-infested, and poorly groomed. What we found here in San Pedro surprised us! That was not the case at all. Dogs are also man's best friend in San Pedro, but they are treated differently here. I must admit, I actually liked what I found better than the "pampered pooch" approach to dog care.

Most Belizean families have a dog. Their dogs have a job. They protect the yard, eat the leftovers, and provide companionship to their owners. Generally, dogs do not sleep indoors in this country. Many families let their dogs out to run each morning when they leave for work. It is an island so they can't go anywhere but back home after a long and busy day. Some dogs roam the streets and search for scraps to eat. They run down the beach as if they have a destination, but they are actually out frolicking and stretching their legs after a long night spent guarding the homestead. They swim in the sea and nap in the sand under the shady palms.

The dogs that have owners wear collars. The dogs without collars are, eventually picked-up by the humane society and they are adopted by people around the island. Some visiting gringos have adopted dogs from SAGA Humane Society, the local shelter, and taken them back to Canada or the States.

Here in Belize there is a history of dog lashing. This town has its roots as a fishing community. Each day the fisherman would clean the catch and hang it on boards or lay it out to be dried and salted. The dogs had to be taught at a young age not to eat the catch and this applies to the cats as well. After being disciplined a time or two, the dogs got the hint, and would leave the human food alone. This practice, as harsh as it sounds, has actually kept the island-dogs, very well mannered.

When you encounter dogs on the street, they don't bother you. They don't jump on you, bark at you, they don't whine if their owner goes away, and they don't pester you for attention. They walk freely through the open-air restaurants without stopping to stare, or beg. In most cases they are polite and well mannered compared to American dogs. On the island, the dogs with the least desirable behavior have been owned by Americans and Canadians who tend to spoil their pets tremendously.

Dr. Floyd has a miniature poodle that will not quit barking at high pitch shrieks, and bites hysterically at the leash if Floyd stops for one moment to talk with us. Our realtor has a Chihuahua that yaps non-stop at equally high decibels when she drives it around in her golf cart. Another lady, who is actually a veterinarian, brings her pit-bull into any establishment including restaurants, and it approaches complete strangers and starts licking them like a treat. A restaurant owner brings his huge, fat, smelly, old Rottweiler into businesses and lets her lay on the floor and pant and drool and stink the place up! I could go on and on. The beach dogs rarely cause disturbances. The loose dogs get along and a serious skirmish between them is uncommon.

The dogs here are a funny mix of all breeds. You see an occasional purebred, but it is usually owned by a gringo. In my experience, I have found that mix breeds tend to be healthier and suffer less from genetic flaws than purebred dogs do. The beach dogs are not sickly and mal-nourished as I had expected them to be.

In my last career, involving dog nutrition, I advised my customers that it is not only safe to feed your dog your table scraps, but it is often better for them than the popular dog foods. Dogs are not meant to eat corn and soybeans which is what most dog food is composed of. They are meant to eat meat and bones and a small amount of green vegetables. Local dog owners feed their dogs the scraps from their fish, chicken, rice, and vegetables. Nothing is ever wasted.

The wealthier people are happy to be able to afford "real" dog food (which is made of corn) and they have no idea that they are actually doing their dogs a disservice.

In my observations, the dogs on this island are not starved, flea infested, or desperate animals. They are loved and well cared for. They live their lives protecting the home and running free in the streets while playing with their dog friends. They appear happy in their surroundings, content with their lot in life. The dogs and cats here thrive in the warmth and sunshine. The island police do not enforce leash-laws or barking ordinances to suppress the dogs' free spirits in any way. They are happy and free and living in paradise just as we are! It's still a dog's life, but it's a great one!

The Saga Humane Society deserves an honorable mention here. They try to keep the dog population under control and remove the diseased or nuisance animals from the streets. Many of the island "beach dogs" have not been neutered and indiscriminate breeding is prevalent and leads to drastic steps taken by the local government. The Town Board will occasionally do a mass eradication of stray dogs. A notice is given to the public to keep their pets at home on the designated day. They destroy the animals by leaving poisoned meat around town for the strays to consume and die. Belize is a third-world nation with very few resources to spare and they tend to rely on the "old way" of solving their problems. It's not likely to change soon even though it is a temporary solution to a very old problem. It's an animal advocate's nightmare!

"To be followed home by a stray dog is a sign of impending wealth."

Chinese proverb

Chapter 37

REAL CHARACTERS

I suppose that there are strange and unusual people all over this planet, but this tiny island sure has attracted its fair share of unique characters! I have written about the variety of international travelers that regularly visit Ambergris Caye, and who choose Belize as their vacation destination. A few of the people who chose this island as their permanent home deserve mention as well. Most of them have lived here for more than a decade.

I must start with Coconut Leo! Leo climbs 40' coconut palms every day and gathers fresh coconut-water for sale. He is a Rastafarian, and has won large sums of money singing Bob Marley's songs in local contests. He truly captures the spirit of reggae music, and is an excellent singer and performer. He sometimes climbs down the tall trees upside down as a tourist attraction, and receives generous tips for his efforts. He has made thousands of friends from around the world. You can view him on You-Tube.

Then there is Dr. Floyd Jackson. A highly educated individual who chooses to live in his boat, docked securely on the lagoon side of the island. He has held lofty positions in education here, and is the founder of "The Free School of Music" on the island. Harvard, Yale, and Julliard trained, he is a retired child psychiatrist who will resume his practice in emergencies. An interesting, and knowledgeable conversationalist, you will find him playing his antique violin, or silver flute, at area restaurants on weeknights. He is truly a renaissance man!

We can't forget David the Dog Whisperer. He can often be spotted walking down the beach with five or ten large dogs on leashes. He amazes us with his complete control of large-breed canines! The dogs seem almost in a trance as he exercises them by walking them for miles each day. There must be some unseen communication going on, based on the dogs' perfect behavior. He is completely calm at all times, and the dogs never pull on their leashes. You just gotta' see it to believe it!

And everyone's favorite, "The Cookie Lady." Pamela makes her living on the island by baking banana-bread and chocolate-chunk cookies fresh every day. Nobody can resist her piping-hot breads, muffins, and soft, chocolaty cookies, as she sells her decadent goodies from bar to bar. She gives free cookies to the poor children, and is generous to a fault. Renowned for her delicious treats, the island is a little sweeter because of Pamela!

Lenny, the Wood Carver, and Craft Dealin' Preacher. Any day of the week, you can spot Lenny on his bicycle, coming down the beach, with polished, hand-crafted, hard-wood carvings in his hand. He sells his art to tourists for a very fair price. He is a religious man, and can recite any psalm in the bible, word for word. A conversation with Lenny is guaranteed to lift your spirits and brighten your day!

Clinton Bush, the Bartending Chiropractor. Named like two former U.S. Presidents, Clinton is a true "healer." Most people meet him at the cantina where he works, as they enjoy a tropical drink and the prestidigitation and card tricks that he so aptly performs behind the bar. Soon the conversation leads to your general health, and you find out that he was trained in Chinese medicine for many years. Before you know it, you are stretched out over three bar-stools and he is fixing that glitch in your back, neck, ankle, or knee that has been bothering you for the past twenty years. Although his techniques are a bit unorthodox, you walk away amazed that your problem has suddenly disappeared. No, it wasn't the booze. Clinton Bush is a gifted person, and we are all somehow improved by the experience of knowing him.

Elizabeth, the Karaoke Singer. A shop-owner-by-day from the north island, Elizabeth comes to San Pedro at night to "wow" us with her hobby, karaoke singing! She is a tall and stolid Austrian woman who can shatter a glass with her voice. Her style is unique, and no one, anywhere, sounds like she does. The sincerity and passion captured in her voice will bring tears to your eyes. When we drive by the many karaoke bars in town, we can always tell when Elizabeth is giving her audience her newest interpretation of a popular song. Her voice and Austrian accent are unmistakable, and to hear her sing is an unforgettable experience.

Carol, the Bike Ridin' Chatter-Box! A retired teach from New York, Carol knows what you had for lunch today, if you live on the island. She is like a newspaper when it comes to daily reports about life here on Ambergris Caye. Nothing escapes her ears, and most of that escapes out of her mouth before day's end. If you need to know about anything "island" just ask Carol. She has friends everywhere and collects tid-bits and anecdotes from many anonymous sources. She always has time for a lengthy conversation, and you will receive more than you bargained for if you are interested. She covers miles on her bicycle each day, and there is always a lot of information coming her way. Around here we say "Just ask Carol!"

Dennis Wolfe and Mr. Charlie are rock 'n' roll musicians who came here over 25 years ago. Dennis and Charlie are icons on this island. They both chose beautiful and talented Belizean women to marry, and have worked very hard to create a great life for their families here in san Pedro.

Charlie owns "Estelle's" restaurant, and he is the island's only true musicologist. Renowned for his taste in music, his collection of rare recordings is incredible! He is full of fun stories from the old days here, and always finds time to tell those stories and make us laugh. His restaurant serves the best breakfast on the sea, and a visit with Charlie will fill up your belly, and enlighten your mind.

Dennis Wolfe is a great songwriter, and has the best band in San Pedro. He works seven nights a week entertaining tourists and locals with his vast repertoire of songs. A visit to the island must include a night with Dennis Wolfe and the Usual Suspects. You will hear great music that will make you dance, sing, and smile all night long!

The newest "Suspect" in Dennis Wolfe's band is Miss Sherry. Discovering the bass guitar after many careers, she quickly mastered the instrument and found her passion singing classic rock-n-roll. She is a feisty Canadian transplant to San Pedro and is known to change her hair color on a weekly basis. Always in the avant garde she is a trend setter with a keen sense of fashion and reinvents her look on a weekly schedule. We recognize Sherry for her vigorous energy and her dazzling style! Flamboyant with lots of flair, she brings "pizzazz" to Ambergris Caye!

Vince and Cherie of A.C.E.S. (American Crocodile Education Sanctuary) are a courageous couple who risk their lives for the conservation of Belize's wetland habitats and the protection of species, specifically crocodiles. Not only do they protect the animals but also the residents of

Ambergris Caye by relocating potentially dangerous crocodiles that may threaten people or their pets. On a typical rescue/relocation job, brave Cherie tapes a thirteen foot crocodile's mouth shut and ties it up as Vince pins the wily creature to the ground. Vince is truly a real life Dundee" down here in Belize!

The "ceviche sisters." Everyone here knows ten year-old Blanca and her twelve year-old sister, Samantha. They canvas the island with their mom seven nights a week, selling the ceviche that they make fresh every day. It is delicious! It is almost impossible to refuse it when the girls flash their beaming smiles and offer it for sale. They dress in their best clothes and are extremely polite children. The profit from their sales goes to their family, helping six brothers and sisters survive in a place with few paying jobs. If you visit the island and go out at night, you will meet them. Pity the fool who doesn't give their ceviche a try!

"Aunty Em!" from Kansas City, KS. Emma is a strong individual who escaped an impoverished upbringing and achieved her dream of living on an island. She moved to San Pedro on her own when she was fifty-seven shears old. Emma learned to use a sewing machine shortly after learning to walk. She is an industrious hard-working entrepreneur and used her skills as a seamstress to make her mark in the world. She creates her entire wardrobe and designs custom clothes for others. You can spot her blocks away by her signature hats.

She was nicknamed "la ballerina" twelve years ago by Dennis Wolfe's son Dennisito. He was the drummer in his father's band and Emma would dance gracefully and artistically during the band's performances at "The Hideaway." Emma learned to dance for physical therapy to help her recover from a devastating car accident and when you watch her pirouette across the dance floor, it is obvious that her recovery is complete.   She is extremely knowledgeable and can discuss almost any topic! An avid reader and intellectual, she is a walking encyclopedia who will happily share her experiences with you. A short conversation with Emma will expand your vocabulary, improve your memory, refresh your table manners, and rekindle your love of books and reading! An interesting character indeed, we welcome her as SierraSky's surrogate grandmother. We need more Emmas in the world!

Fishman Johnson, the "go-to" guy for fish! If you are looking for a fresh catch and aren't sure where to begin, ask for the "Fishman." Although he moves around from various storefronts to obscure vegetable stands to ply his wares, you can ask just about anyone where he is on a given day. From Nicaraguan jumbo shrimp to Chilean sea bass he has connections for fresh seafood that no one else seems to have. Yellow-fin tuna, barracuda, billfish, grouper, snappers, lobster, blue crab, black-fin tuna, Spanish mackerel, skipjack tuna, bonefish, Snook, tarpon, and Wahoo, are all available if you order ahead. His prices are fair and his personality is priceless! Your seafood dream will come true if you run into Fishman Johnson!

Pirate! Aaaaarrrgh! An imposing and intimidating figure with his black wardrobe, shaved head, black hat, tattoos and gold earring; the nickname of "Pirate" fits him well. Pirate is in charge of the color black here in San Pedro. Riding around the island in his black four-wheeler with a skull and crossbones flag flying high, it is impossible to miss him. It turns out that Dennis comes from Kenosha, Wisconsin, and we knew many of the same people growing up. He is a kind and gentle soul and a notoriously grumpy old man. Pirate continues to hang on to the all-time record at BC's Friday Night Trivia hosted by Carlo!

There you have it, a snapshot of seventeen unusual people who add flavor to the island with their uniqueness and their charm. We will "A crane standing amidst a flock of chickens." Chinese proverb

Chapter 38

LIVING IN A TOURIST TOWN

When we lived in Wisconsin we certainly had our fare share of tourism. Each June we saw the city of Lake Geneva fill up with people escaping from Chicago for the week-end, or choosing our beautiful blue lake as the destination for their summer vacation. In a typical year of tourism the population would go from five thousand residents to fifty thousand guests by mid-summer. We were thankful for the money they spent in our little town and we gladly cleaned up the trash the tourists left behind. After Labor Day, we saw the tourist traffic come to a screeching halt when school started up again.

Most of the tourists in Lake Geneva were people from Chicago or its suburbs. Only 90 minutes away, it was easy for someone to jump in their car and speed along the super highway, cross the

Illinois/Wisconsin border, and coast into Lake Geneva. They tended to be people who are rather caught up in fast boats, fancy cars, expensive jewelry, painted nails, etc. Big spenders who knew how to have a good time!

Now we find ourselves living in another tourist destination. Happily for us, this time around it is a very different experience. It is a little harder to get to San Pedro, and it attracts a diverse crowd. People come from all over the world. There are plenty of Canadians, Texans, New Yorkers, many wealthy Mexicans, South and Central Americans, and a steady flow of tourists from England, as Belize is still in the Commonwealth and probably always will be. Most people come here for the best diving anywhere, the Mayan ruins, a jungle adventure, or to just enjoy the tropical paradise that is Belize. There is plenty to see and do here, and it would take a lifetime to do it all.

Robert and I never met many Chicago tourists even though we were surrounded by thousands of them each summer. They are a bit distant and generally un-approachable. It's what big-city life does to you, I suppose. Here in San Pedro Town we seem to meet interesting and memorable people every week. The Belizean's laid-back style and friendly ways tend to rub off on you. When you stop to ask a Belizean a question, you often find yourself in a long, relaxed conversation. Not just a quick answer and then back to what they were doing. They always seem to have time to offer help and a cheerful word. After a few days in Belize, I think the tourists slow down, switch gears, open up a little, and take the time to enjoy the island rhythms and to really appreciate the friendliness of the people around them.

I am sure that this has rubbed off on us as well. We now take the time to talk, to hear what people are saying, to notice the subtleties of life by slowing it down. It is routine here to share stories and smiles, insights and laughter, heartfelt concerns, adventuresome thrills, and then have our new acquaintances go back from where they came, usually in 7-10 days. We would swap emails and hope to keep in touch until they come back the next year, which so many of them do. When people discover Belize, many of them are determined to return. Jerry Jeff sings about it in his song "Come away to Belize" He says, "Your heart never leaves, once you've been down to Belize."

What a special privilege to accumulate friends from around the world. We played guitars and sang with Gary from Oregon. We sailed around the islands with Ross & Eve from Canada. We partied with Wendy in her fabulous condo at The Phoenix, the top hotel on the island. Wendy holds the record so far. She has flown here three times in five weeks from Brooklyn, New York!

We enjoyed a delicious lobster dinner with a Japanese photographer, Steve, who was visiting from Los Angeles. We dined with a young couple from Michigan, Tom and Stacy who were E.R. doctors. Ken and Melissa are from Indiana and they can dance all night long. He is the spitting image of Tom Bosely, the dad in Happy Days.

We met a man named Terry (his wife is also Teri!) who is in the front lines of growing medical marijuana in Marin County California. He has chosen an interesting line of work. We shared our catamaran trip to Caye Caulker with friends from Arizona, Jeanine who is a painter of nude models and her friend Chuck, a young man who owns his own small aircraft transport company. They were a barrel of laughs!

The very first couple we met here were Colin and Libby. We dined with them on a rainy night at Caramba's and discovered that they were from the United Kingdom and had stopped in Belize as they were making their way down to the southern tip of Argentina by bus. They had come across Canada and made their way down the

Pacific coast highway. What an adventure they were on...

We have been privileged to meet people from Europe, Panama, Columbia, Peru, Guatemala, Ecuador, Mexico and Honduras.

San Pedro Town also brings in groups of people. For example there is a club called "Dive Belize." You would think this was probably a scuba diving group but it is a group of skydivers. Of course Jerry Jeff Walker comes here every year with "Camp Belize," and attracts a huge crowd of wealthy Texas yuppies who definitely know how to have fun! Various charitable clubs have come as well, including a group of dentists who came and donated their skills at the least privileged school on the island. A church group of teenagers came here for a month and built a new playground for the kids.

We also have the annual Costa Maya Festival, a beauty pageant in San Pedro, featuring gorgeous young ladies who represent every country in Central America. At dinner one evening, SierraSky was fortunate enough to have her photo taken with the contestants gathered all around her. They were sweethearts and happily posed with our daughter.

It has been interesting and exciting meeting new people and making new friends. Tropic Air and Maya Island Air bring several loads of tourists to San Pedro every day of the week. It is a small island and we eventually run into most of them before their week here is over. It would be impossible to name everyone that we have shared time with. Each person, couple, or family was a delight in their own way, and we are looking forward to their return to paradise. We will be right here, waiting with open arms!

"Treat your guest like a guest for three days, then give him a hoe"

Chinese proverb

Chapter 39

"SHARK" ATTACK

I had a wild experience! I was enjoying my daily swim at the end of Wet Willy's dock with SierraSky and Emma. It was a typical swim and we all had our goggles, fins, and snorkel gear. We were casually observing the fish under the pier. This is a very pleasurable way to spend a couple of hours. SierraSky had finally become an expert swimmer and I no longer worried about her safety. I could actually swim around a bit, follow the interesting fish that catch my eye, and give an occasional glance in her direction to see if she is all right.

I was about 20 feet away from SierraSky and the ladder, when I noticed some little floating objects that reminded me of tiny jellyfish. I remember pausing in the water and staring up at the surface into the sunlight, looking at these strange colorful little blobs. Out of nowhere, this weird looking and unfamiliar fish swam directly at me! I was immediately alarmed because fish never swim towards me, they are experts at swimming away from people. I have become very comfortable swimming right into schools of fish because I know that they will somehow always avoid me. It is such a natural feeling being in the water among the fish, I almost felt like one myself.

I was perplexed to see this fish approaching my mask. It was long, cylindrical, grey with hints of black, and a white belly. It had a big head. It looked just like a baby hammer-head shark. This peculiar fish was only about eight inches long, but I became suddenly very frightened and uncomfortable! When I realized it was coming for me, and definitely not changing course, I swam like an Olympian to the ladder. I didn't look forward, and I couldn't look back as I crashed into SierraSky and the pier at full force! I quickly proceeded to drag SierraSky out of the water while trampling over the local Belizean boys who were hanging on the ladder. I screamed, "A baby shark is after me!" They were laughing as I jumped up on the dock. I never expected that I would be so frightened while swimming. This fish was aggressive and I was sure that it was definitely after me.

The boys quickly looked around but didn't see it. I'm sure they thought I must be crazy. When I crashed into the ladder I got scratched by the barnacles and was bleeding. This really enhanced the story that I told Robert about my "shark" attack. It all happened so fast that I needed a moment to gather myself. I knew that a baby hammerhead has to be born larger than eight inches. I had to find out what kind of fish that was to put my mind at ease.

I went back to the pier to look around in the water hoping to see the fish again. I knew I probably wouldn't get a second look at it. As I walked back down the long pier to shore I saw the divers at Reef Adventure's dive shop. I told them about my experience, and asked them what they thought the fish was. They hemmed and hawed for a while, and then agreed on a species. They decided it must have been a remora or a suckerfish. A remora is a fish that clings to sharks and other large fish and cleans them. When it saw me, it must have mistaken me for a big fish, and wanted to attach itself to me!

It was all so innocent. The little fish just wanted to clean me. It was kind of silly and non-threatening but it managed to scare the heck out of me! I did exactly what you're not supposed to do when you see a shark; I swam in a panic and splashed up a storm in my haste to escape! I'll try to do better in future trials, and remain calm. Imagine if I had just floated there without reacting, and the remora attached itself to me? I would have really freaked-out!

I am learning to cautiously enjoy my new home, and deal with all of its surprises and un-perceived dangers.

"If you stand straight, do not fear a crooked shadow."

Chinese Proverb

Chapter 40

HURRICANE SEASON

I had never experienced a full-blown tropical cyclone and I often wondered what it was like to be in a hurricane. Two-thirds of the way through the hurricane season there had been five "near-misses" as Hurricanes Alex, Karl, Mathew, Paula and Richard brushed past our tiny island.

The first storm of the year was a tropical depression and wasn't even a named storm. It came from the Pacific Ocean. It raged over Guatemala and the winds from it shook our house to the foundation. The rain was incredible! It broke the record on Ambergris Caye with the most rainfall in 24 hours. It went on to the U.S. and caused major flooding in Nashville.

The first named tropical storm was Alex, and it developed in the

Caribbean Sea right off the coast of Belize. We didn't know how fast it would grow or if it would head towards us or move north to the Yucatan. After the house-shaking from a mere tropical depression, we were concerned.

We prepared for the worst. We saw our neighbors boarding up their windows, and soon realized that this was a standard precaution. We kept a radar vigil. It didn't look like it would form into a hurricane before reaching Belize, so we didn't leave the island. We cleared our yard of any objects that could be picked up by the wind and turn into projectiles that may cause injuries or damage. We stocked up on our canned goods, batteries, candles, water and entertainment supplies, and sat on the porch until the rains came. There were very strong winds that night and several trees, roofs, and signs came down in San Pedro Town. I have experienced July thunderstorms in Wisconsin with stronger gusts than tropical storm Alex created. Two days later, Alex was upgraded to hurricane status after passing over us.

The next storm was hurricane Karl, which also formed off the coast of Belize in the Caribbean Sea. We were fortunate to have Mr. Frank Panton nearby. He works with NEMO, and has the final word on hurricane preparedness in Belize. He is highly respected and appreciated for his efforts. Anytime there is a storm approaching, Frank is all over the TV and radio stations with the newest update on the impending storm. We get the inside scoop on what is developing. He advises us to make our own choice, but he lets us know any information that may be helpful in making our decision whether to stay here or leave the island.

In its final approach to the island, Karl didn't appear too threatening so we stayed home again. The low impact of the first storm helped us to be a little more relaxed this time. We didn't stock up on supplies and we didn't strap down the propane tank or the golf-cart. Karl brought us heavy winds, and some heavy rains.

I am finding that the storms in Wisconsin were actually more dangerous and unexpected. Tornadoes form in minutes and cause devastating damage. We had three tornadoes touch-down near our home town of Lake Geneva in one week a couple of years ago.

The Wisconsin thunderstorm knocked a monstrous sugar-maple tree onto our fence, and the wind blew a window and its trim off of our house. We had no warning about the wind gusts, even with Doppler radar in Milwaukee. Atlantic hurricanes, are carefully tracked, and monitored long before they become tropical storms. There is plenty of advance notice to prepare for a hurricane.

We were getting used to these tropical storms by the time Matthew came through. We weren't expecting much more than wind and rain. Since we were not living on the low side of the island we weren't concerned about flooding. Matthew packed a surprise for us! It was still a tropical storm when it hit Nicaragua, the country just south of Belize. Severe rain damage, flooding, and mud-slides occurred. The storm made the ocean rise to unexpected heights with the storm-surge. On Ambergris Caye, the waves beyond the reef looked like they were twenty feet tall! The barrier reef kept the high waves out to sea. By the time the waves rolled over it and came to shore they were only about five feet tall. The usually gentle and calm coastline is not used to much wave action, especially waves of that height! Matthew went on to become the 4th deadliest hurricane of the season and caused a major landslide in Mexico, burying over 300 homes.

The waves were coming up through the wooden planks of the docks and many piers lost their boards. Chuck and Robbie's, the fishing and dive shop in front of our house, was in danger of being swept away all together. The owners and employees were frantically removing everything from the office on the dock. They didn't expect this kind of wave activity. Usually the fishermen move their boats to the leeward side of the island well in advance of wind and waves. This time the high water level came sooner than expected. The fishing boats were battling the five foot waves as they tried to go around to the lagoon where the water is calmer.

The sea swelled over the beach in front of our house and everyone was moving their golf carts and bringing their smaller boats as high on the beach as possible. The waves covered the beach road but didn't quite make it up to our fence. The water deposited copious amounts of sea grass and fish onto the beach.

When the storm subsided we went for a walk to see the damage left in the wake of hurricane Mathew. We found a young parrot fish on the road in a puddle. It was still alive and a young boy put it back in the sea. We were happy to see it swim away. We saw hermit crabs that had crawled into the trees to protect themselves from the rough sea. We also found many great treasures such as brain coral, sea fans, pretty shells and other types of interesting souvenirs that had washed onto the beach.

The next morning the beach was so clean it was hard to believe that there was a major storm the day before. Workers arrived early and raked the sea grass into big piles. They dug large pits in the sand and buried it. This is how they build up the beach and other low spots on the island.

Hurricane Paula passed us by. Unbelievably, it remained sunny and warm, and there were no clues that a storm of its size was just a hundred miles north of Ambergris Caye. When the emergency had passed, it was business as usual on the island.

We learned many valuable lessons while witnessing these storms, and the human response to this type of emergency. It is uplifting to see neighbors come together in the wake of potential disaster.

People put aside their differences and help each other board-up windows. It is also interesting to see the scramble when the "me first" side of human nature comes out at the grocery store, the water taxi, the airports. Some people are scared to death while others are filled with excitement. Some retreat to safety with their bible, others gather for a party with extra rum. With just six weeks to go in the hurricane season, we hoped that our luck would continue. Would there be another hurricane?

"The day's fortunes are no more to be told than the weather."

Chinese proverb

Chapter 41

HURRICANE RICHARD ARRIVES

We had been dodging bullets all summer and fall, as hurricane after hurricane blew past us. Living here on the island felt like being a pin in a bowling alley! It was just a matter of time until the "big one" hit us. We had been fortunate so far as the storms passed one hundred miles from us, or were still in the tropical storm stage when they arrived here. Our luck finally ran out on October 25th with Hurricane Richard.

When hurricanes Alex, Matthew, Karl & Paula came through here, we didn't take things too seriously. We had grown used to the storms not being much of a threat, fifty mph winds at best. It seemed like the media was blowing things out of proportion and we were becoming a bit complacent. As we watched Hurricane Richard develop in the Caribbean Sea, the media predicted a direct hit on Belize. We changed our tune. It was time to get ready for a big hurricane.

The weathermen and newscasters have to rally people to take hurricanes and tropical storms very seriously in the hope that they will possibly save lives and property. The worst possible outcome does not happen every time. It is very hard to predict when it will. A hurricane under perfect conditions can grow 10 times its size in just a few short hours.

I started to get nervous as I watched the storm on television and on my computer. Robert was cool as a cucumber. He had been studying the radar, water temperatures, pressure gradients, and the various factors that make these storms increase rapidly. He seemed confident that it would be smaller than the media stated, and hopefully miss us like the last four major storms had.

We asked our good friend Frank Panton, the meteorologist, what he thought Richard would do. He predicted that it would be a direct hit on Belize and that it could be as much as a Category 2.

Frank always stays on the island to instruct the evacuation crews and various assistance groups who stay to help during the storm. His wife happened to be out of the country on business. Our original plan had been that if Frank decided that any storm looked like it would be dangerous enough to send his family elsewhere, we would leave the island as well. Since she was already out of the country, and the storm was headed towards us, we needed to come up with a new plan.

I made some phone calls to the airlines and priced out the cheapest flight we could get to leave Belize. I found out was that there weren't any flights available. All flights were booked months in advance by travelers who had planned trips for that particular day. Extra flights are filled by evacuated tourists. The travel agent informed me that If there are no seats left people go to a "hurricane-proof" hotel and ride out the storm.

We discovered that there are many hotels in San Pedro that are built to withstand large storms, and they used to provide a room at a discounted price at the last minute! Now we find that things have changed. The hotels are required to release employees from their jobs and therefore, there is no one to run the hotel and it has to close.

As Hurricane Richard approached, it became apparent that it was heading straight for us! On the day of Richard's predicted arrival, SierraSky was busy playing with the video camera. She asked me to video tape her as she stood in front of the television and pretended to be a newscaster, with the coverage of hurricane Richard on the Weather Channel behind her. She was funny, but it still didn't distract me from my concern about how serious this storm was going to be. The unpredictability of the storm's exact landfall and intensity was unnerving.

I spoke with my friend Emma who watches and tracks the weather almost as much as Frank. She was cool like Robert. She felt that the storm was going to hit south of us and since it was not very wide, it wouldn't become much worse than it already was. This made me feel a little more relaxed, as I watched it approach on the radar screen!

The wind was blowing, the sea was rising, and gigantic waves were crashing loudly out on the reef. The atmosphere was electrifying! Everyone was scurrying about getting last minute supplies.

Our landlord came by and asked if we wanted him to board-up the windows right away? I thought it was odd that would he ask us. It was our first actual hurricane, and we had carefully studied hurricane preparedness, but we were certainly no experts on what needed to be done.

Robert was still confident with his sources of information and said, "No thank you, that probably won't be necessary." I interrupted and I said "Actually, I would feel much better if you do. There is a dead palm tree in the neighbor's yard and I would hate to see it fall over and break a window or something." The two men had a laugh about how silly their wives are when they worry so much, and the landlord said he would send someone over to board us up.

A few hours passed by and the wind was steadily picking up speed. It was getting later in the day and no one came with any plywood. I became anxious and felt that we should go to a concrete building instead of staying in our wooden beach house. Our "Plan B" was that if we didn't leave the island, we would stay at a hotel or at our friend Miss Monica's condo. She had mentioned in the past that we were welcome to come to her house in the case of a hurricane. She is also rather complacent about the tropical storms based on her experiences here on the island. When I called Monica she was not only welcoming, but insistent that we come to her safe shelter.

Robert politely declined. It had become too windy and rainy to move our valuables out of the house. He wanted to stay and protect our guitars and belongings in case there were any looters about.

SierraSky and I packed a bag. At this point we still didn't know how severe the storm was going to be. I was unsure of what to take with us, or how much to bring along for a potentially prolonged stay. I packed candles, flashlights, a blow-up mattress, some toiletries, clothes, snacks, a book, some kid games and cards, and a bottle of good Caribbean rum to take the edge off. Can you imagine how much that weighs? I hadn't thought about it until I lifted our fully-packed bag. It must have weighed over 50 pounds! I lugged it over to Miss Monica's apartment with our daughter in tow.

Just as SierraSky and I were leaving, the workmen arrived with the plywood covers for the windows. They had to climb on ladders in the rain and the wind and struggle with these heavy and clumsy big boards. Lesson learned? If you think there is going to be a direct hit from a hurricane, put the boards up the day before! Our neighbors were also scrambling at the last minute to put up their metal hurricane shutters. I always wondered if there was an easy and simple way to board up a house, but from what I saw, that was not the case. It looked like difficult work to do on a good day, much less in the rain and wind. I am sure that there are modern techniques and systems, but they are not being used in our neighborhood. Somehow, with super-human effort, the workmen completed the job.

We couldn't hear the storm at all once we were inside Monica's apartment. We turned on the news and saw that the eye of the storm was hitting Belize at that moment. It came ashore just 40 miles south of us, near Belize City. Richard was upgraded to a category two hurricane. It was expected that the tail end of the storm was going to hit the island later that evening around 10 pm, and we remembered that the last part of the storm is often the strongest.

It was around 5pm when we went to Monica's. We all played games and ate cookies, and had fun passing the time. It was a very pleasant evening but it was not exactly the "hurricane party" I had pictured in my mind after hearing stories from our friends on the island.

The storm seemed to be waning instead of increasing. I called Robert to see how the storm was progressing on the beach. We were aware that the water could surge into our yard. He reported that it hadn't made it to the street. He said that it wasn't raining anymore and that the wind had decreased to 40mph.

Hurricane Matthew was much worse with its huge swells, torrential rains, and storm surge. Instead of spending a fear-filled sleepless night at Monica's, with the wind howling and windows rattling, we packed our super heavy survival bag and headed back home at 8pm. The storm steadily weakened. We sat on our front porch enjoying the sound of wind and waves. Robert and Emma were correct about its benign climax. A direct hit from hurricane Richard skirted by us. Our luck held out after all.

That was not the case for Belize City. There was massive damage from flooding and the rain totals were the highest in recent memory! With over $160 million dollars in damage, and still counting, many families suffered as Richard rolled across Belize. We heard remarks that the storm helped clean up Belize City. Someone observed, "Hurricane Richard provided a thorough washing that was long overdue."

It is very important for the officials and newscasters to continually caution us to take these massive storms seriously. The drama created by the media, still outweighs the impact of many of these storms. It only takes one devastating storm to make you appreciate what all the hype is about. The National Hurricane Center called off the hurricane season fifteen days early. We had seen enough for our first hurricane season.

"When storm comes, some build higher walls while others build wind mills."

Chinese proverb

Chapter 42

RETURN OF THE SNOWBIRDS

In the second week of November the "snowbirds" begin their migration to Ambergris Caye. There are fresh gringos filling the streets, hotels, restaurants and bars again. They stick out like sore thumbs. The most recent group of tourists tend to be pale, stressed-out, and pre-occupied by things left un-done back home. They gaze around with their mouths agape and appear lost, disoriented, and stunned by the sudden halt of the rush-rush pace that they have become accustomed to in the United States. On or around day three, you can see them start to slow down, relax, unwind, and let go of the stress that big-city living creates. The look in their eyes tells us they are keenly aware that all-too-soon, they will return to their busy lives.

The locals are happy to see our vacationing visitors return.

Tourism is the life-blood of this tiny island. Money arrives from other countries in the pockets of snorkelers, scuba enthusiasts, and sport fisherman. There are hundreds of San Pedranos employed by the diving trade, and at least another 2,500 work in hospitality. The fishing and diving "deals" are everywhere you look and competition keeps the prices affordable. The hotels and restaurants welcome visitors with the 'red-carpet' treatment. Belizeans are trained from childhood to be polite to adults and elders. When the newest guests arrive here they are treated with respect and referred to as "Sir" or "Boss," or "Mr. Rob and "Miss Lydia."

After living on the island for a year, it became harder for us to remember that we were once snowbirds ourselves. The return of the tourists to Ambergris Caye reminds us that our dream came true. We now take pride in the fact that we are actually living here and we share the responsibility of giving a warm Belizean welcome to new and returning vacationers.

"How happy to have friends from far away!"

Confucius

Chapter 43

EVERYTHING FALLS INTO PLACE

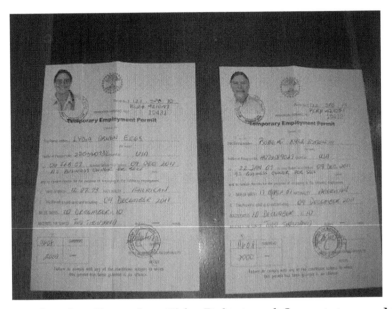

On Wednesday December 7'th, Robert and I went to see Mr. George at the Labor Department. With a beaming smile Mr. George reported the news that Belmopan had approved us for our work permits! I remember expecting that he would hand over a certificate or form of some kind but he just sat there and smiled at us. I broke the silence by saying "Do we get a card or something?" He chuckled and said, "No. Go to the Department of Immigration, tell them you have been approved and they will send you to the Treasurer where you will pay $1000.00 USD each. Be sure to get a receipt. Then go back to the Department of Immigration to receive a stamp in your passport with the work permit number on it. Finally, bring your passports and receipt back to me and I will issue your official work permit document."

We went straight to the Department of Immigration. We were surprised when they told us that they had not received *their* copy of the notification letter from Belmopan and could not stamp our passports yet. We said "Well, Mr. George said he received one, can you call him?" Their response was a matter-of-fact, "Nope." We went home with mixed feelings of joy and disappointment. We were learning to have more patience with the way things are done in Belize and told ourselves "It will happen when it happens."

The next morning an older lady that I had met in the local women's card group came over to our house. I was very surprised because people here do not usually show up unexpectedly. I was in the shower at the time but I could tell that whoever was knocking on the door was determined to get an answer. I wrapped myself in a robe and answered the door. When I saw eighty-five year old Marge standing there I thought "What on earth could this be about?"

Marge asked to come in because she had something important to tell us. She knew from the card group chatter that my husband and I play instruments, and that we intended to start performing live music around town. She lived next door to a vacationing couple who happened to be the parents of the managers of Wet Willy's Cantina. She heard that they were ready to move on in life and that they were looking for a team to replace them in their jobs after five years of hard work. Marge had come over to tell me that she thought Robert and I would be perfect for the position and that we could kick-start our musical careers right there on the dock!

We had already decided to avoid stressful, demanding jobs. Managing a bar was at the bottom of our list. With her enthusiasm and encouragement, Marge made it sound fun and easy. We considered her message. Wet Willy's was our favorite nightspot on the island. As the year went by, we watched as business slowed and eventually the bar closed for ten weeks. Robert and I had been sitting on our front porch, playing our guitars and staring at Wet Willy's day after day. We had been speculating how we might bring some business back to the dock if we were running it. Could the law of attraction be in effect here?

We realized that the Department of Labor may make our career decision for us again. We headed over to talk with Mr. George. We explained to him that we were considering the position in management of a bar and restaurant. If we were to accept the job, would we have to start our work permit process from the beginning? George smiled and asked "Can you teach music at the bar?" We said "Yes." He responded "Well, you're good then." Finally, something had gone smoothly and quickly in Belize. The "force was with us."

With the good news from George we headed over to the Department of Immigration hoping for the best. The notification letter had arrived and they gave us more good news! We would no longer have to pay the $100 monthly visa stamps. The work permit replaced this requirement for one year. We paid $2000 USD to the Treasurer and took our receipt to Mr. George. He flashed us his friendly gold-toothed grin, as he handed us our official Belizean work permits!

After a brief talk with Kayleen and Garrick, some deliberation and serious consideration, we applied for the job. We emailed our resume's to the owner of Wet Willy's and offered our skills and expertise as the new management team.

"Don't stand by the water and long for fish; go home and weave a net."

Chinese proverb

Chapter 44

The Time of Observation Comes to an End

After our vacation to Belize we understood what Jerry Jeff was singing about in "Cowboy Boots and Bathing Suits." We played the CD every day to keep the memories of the island lifestyle fresh in our minds and to keep our dream of moving to Belize alive…and before too long we had actually moved here. Dreams do come true!

Sometimes we wonder about "the natural course of events." If we had listened to this CD before we had actually come to Belize and experienced the island firsthand, would it have had the same impact on our lives? Life is peculiar in this way. It seems the timing in our universe is always perfect with the "plan" unfolding exactly as it should. (pause here for deep thoughts…)

We seem to have completed a circle of some kind. On January 1'st, the owner of Wet Willy's Cantina sent us the great news that we had been selected, and HIRED for the management position at his palapa bar!

Wet Willy's was our first destination on the island. In the coming season, WE will be throwing Jerry Jeff's annual concert bash during "Camp Belize!" It is amazing how fantastic things worked out for us!

As Joni Mitchell so aptly put it in her 1970 song:

"And the seasons, they go round and round. And the painted ponies go up and down. We're captive on the carousel of time…We can't return, we can only look, behind from where we came. And go round, and round, and round, in the "Circle Game."

"One meets his destiny often in the road he takes to avoid it"
Chinese proverb.

Chapter 45

"Written On the Skein of Time and Space"

The great sages of history concur on the concept that if every sound emitted from our wondrous planet could be heard at once, we would hear "OM," the sound of the energy of peace. The combined audio vibration of singing voices, music of every description, the squeal of braking tires, babies crying, song-birds chirping, roaring engines, wind whistling in the treetops, volcanoes erupting, lovers whispering, the wails of the suffering, the pure joy of laughter...well, you get the idea. All of these sounds together make a single sound of their own. It is the sound made by earth and its inhabitants, and the sum of all these sounds together, produce a soothing peaceful vibration.

This may seem hard to believe considering that our world appears to be spinning totally out of control, a little more every day. We hear very little about unselfish acts of heroism, philanthropy, and compassionate generosity because it seldom makes the headlines. We blame the news media for this as they compete for ratings.

Back in Wisconsin, our family had become acutely aware of the stressful environment that we lived in. We found ourselves at a place in time where sensationalism and negative headlines seemed to overwhelm us, and the result was that we began to lose sight of what was good and right about our world. Horror movies and dramas with gratuitous graphic violence had begun to out-sell all of the family movies combined. We were immersed in negativity and we yearned for a way out of the darkness that surrounded us. We realized that we needed to take action and remove ourselves from an unhealthy and unpleasant situation in the U.S. Finding a new place to live and raise our child appeared to be the only solution for us, and it became our priority.

The adage, "Life is short" was permeating our thoughts. How did we really want to raise our young daughter? It was unlikely that we would change the superficial values that were gaining strength on a daily basis in the United States.

In linear time, we enjoy a relatively short sojourn on this tiny blue dot in space that we call home. Our planet is circling the sun at an un-godly speed, approximately 67,000 mph, and none of us know how many days we have left in our lives, "that we can truly call our own." Many people nowadays feel a powerful inner urging in the direction of a happier and more peaceful life. We decided to do whatever was required of us to satisfy our innate desire to find that peace, and to make it our reality.

Moving our family to San Pedro Town was the result of our search for serenity, and a simpler way to live. After visiting here the first time, we felt renewed. The dream-like atmosphere of this island improves the quality of life almost immediately. It has a vibration that is harmonious, calm and steady, without all of the pretension found at a typical yoga class or a pay-by-the-week retreat. Aside from the natural beauty of this place, there is a deeper under-current, something unseen and unspoken all around us. Frequently, it feels like a holy place replete with shrines, churches, and meditation enclaves. Could we have stumbled upon one of the "earth energy vortexes" that exist on this planet? It has a powerful "frequency," or "wavelength" that cannot be ignored by anyone who visits here, no matter how briefly. It just plain feels good to be here.

We have speculated that the vibratory anomaly that we sense on this island is somehow connected to the Mayan ruins recently discovered on South Ambergris Caye, just five miles from San Pedro. The Marco Gonzales Ruins site was first documented in 1984. Excavation began in 1994 and many visitors return from the site with stories about how "The feeling you are left with after visiting the Mayan ruins borders on a mystical experience." or, "There is something undeniably ethereal about that site and the aura that surrounds it."

It is difficult to explain what it is that attracts certain people here, but many vacationers want to return to the island and set up permanent households after visiting Isla Bonita just one time. We have personally experienced this phenomenon, and found ourselves compelled to follow enigmatic signposts until we reached our destination.

A unique collection of artists live on Ambergris Caye today. It has attracted transplants from diverse walks of life. Among them are movie directors, poets, playwrights, actors, musicians, artists, painters, fashion designers, jewelry makers, architects, dramatists, authors, world renowned chefs, millionaires who made their money in computers and software, and we even have a rocket scientist living up the coast.

There is something extraordinary, inspiring, and attractive about this location. It is elusive and intangible, yet it is intriguing. I must apologize here for using a word that has been abused, over-used, and often in recent years, has lost its true meaning in the process. The word is "spiritual." There is no other way to describe it. This is a spiritual place. Authentic, bona-fide, and genuine, it is where we chose to re-awaken our eternal selves to what we consider to be the important stuff of life. There is always time for meditative thought in San Pedro...

"Just as a candle cannot burn without fire, men cannot live without a   spiritual   life."
                                                              Buddha

Chapter 46

A YEAR GONE BY

We have seen every aspect of the different seasons; each one beautiful in its own way. We have met hundreds of people coming and going, and a thousand more who live here. We have become familiar with the stores, the restaurants, the postal system, the banks, and we have settled in. Belize is everything we hoped it would be, and more than we dreamed it could be.

Our first year on the island had passed rather quickly and we were feeling sentimental because the holiday season was fast approaching. After a year of eating fish, lobster, and seafood we began to miss our traditional turkey dinner on Thanksgiving. A week before the holiday we received an invitation from Wayne & Jo Castleberry to join them for the annual "gringo Thanksgiving dinner" held in their home. It was an honor to be asked because it meant acceptance into the island family. We were happy to join the festivities and offered to bring the beer.

We met many new friends at this event and feasted on traditional foods that were provided by our hosts. Everyone brought side dishes and cold libations. The roast turkey, smoked glazed ham, green bean casseroles, mashed potatoes and gravy, cranberry sauce, sweet potatoes, candied yams, Caesar salad, and an array of mouth-watering pies and desserts were an epicurean's delight.

We have completed our first year on Ambergris Caye, the "Jewel of Belize." We share a feeling of great accomplishment after jumping through so many hoops. We have surmounted all of the obstacles, hurdles, and various challenges that we could not have anticipated. Now we can apply for our residency.

We acquired great jobs and we are still living in the home we love. It didn't sell! We adopted a kitten for SierraSky and she has more playmates than ever before. When we drive down the streets of San Pedro town she calls out "Hello's" to all of her acquaintances. SierraSky has picked up the local Belizean accent. The next time you speak to her, you will wonder which country she is from. The accent is a mix of Kriol, Mestizo, Spanish, Garifuna, and the "King's English." It is darling. She debates with her Papa whether to pronounce it as "snack" or "snahk." Robert and I are beyond the age of picking up a new accent but we gained much more.

We had been "on a mission to discover what's in the air" in Belize that has such a positive effect on its society. We have truly uncovered the Belizean secret and found it is much more than what's in the air. Each day we become a little more Belizean. We have adopted the slow pace that is "Island time." Our skin is brown in color from all of the vitamin D that we soaked up in the plentiful sunshine. Lately, our smiles and laughter come more easily as we are surrounded by all of the children and child-like teasing among adults. Our bodies have become healthier from our new diet of fresh fish, fruit, and rice and beans. The extra walking in our daily lives strengthened our muscles and the beauty surrounding us strengthened our souls. We have become more relaxed after countless hours spent hanging in hammocks and swimming in the sea. Through all of this, we breathed in the fresh Belizean air that nourished our souls.

We have only one serious regret regarding our decision to move to Belize, and that is…that we didn't do it sooner!

"Life is a precious gift. Don't waste it being unhappy, dissatisfied, or anything less than you can be."

anonymous

Appendix I

Not All Hummingbirds and Butterflies...
Part One

We received an email from friends announcing that they were planning to move to the tropics! We were very excited for them, and happy that beautiful Belize was on their list of possible locations. It is going to be a fun conversation as we discuss the finer points of living here and answer their list of questions about our new-found Shangri-la. Their inquiries helped us realize that every coin has two sides. We felt obligated to present a realistic snapshot of life on the island. There are a few things that many people may NOT like about living here on Ambergris Caye.

Utopia doesn't exist. There will never be a place that is absolutely perfect in every way. If you choose a location that offers the things you enjoy most in life, then be prepared to make some sacrifices. You will have to tolerate the less attractive aspects of a place, wherever you go.

For example, it gets pretty hot and humid here in Belize. The hottest time is between 1pm and 4 pm. It can hit 89 degrees but the heat-index is higher. Much higher! As high as 115 degrees! As the sun retreats to the western horizon, the island cools down nicely from the sea breeze blowing across the water.

I remember those rare, but always welcome, 82 degree, warm, breezy summer evenings in Wisconsin. Almost every night is like that in Belize. Now that we are fully acclimated to this area, the warmth is just a part of everyday life here. I would take a hot day over a cold one anytime. I hope I never feel cold again in my life. Some people like a cold wind and a hot fire. If you like snow and cold-weather sports, you probably would not be happy in Belize without a winter vacation to North America. There are four very distinct seasons here, (Hot, Dry, Wet, & Perfect!) with the temperature never varying more than seven degrees. There is something very happy and pleasant about a perpetual summer…

There are very few beaches in San Pedro Town. When we think of beaches we think of wide stretches of fine sand meeting the waves at the water's edge and unencumbered areas provided for our swimming pleasure. Not here! Beaches average 10 feet wide and there is sea grass growing all along the coast. It is illegal to remove it because it prevents further erosion of this little island. The barrier reef prevents most of the erosion that forms natural beaches and it is only recently that resorts have begun to build their own beaches for tourists to enjoy. The island is so narrow that there is not much room for shoreline to be used for leisure. I have heard that there are some great beaches at the north end of the island and some beautiful romantic strips of sand on the south west side and we look forward to visiting them someday soon.

"The Queen's beach" is what the shoreline is referred to and it comes from a British law made during their 119-years of colonial rule. This law states that all beaches are open to the public and so are all of the docks, even if privately owned. The newly created beaches built by hotels are open to the public much to the owner's dismay.

If you are the type of person that doesn't like air conditioning, you might be frustrated during the summertime in Belize. It has been so hot and humid at times that I am relieved to go into a store that has air conditioning! Turning on the air conditioning has been a blessing at bedtime. The cost of running it all day is not practical. You can ring up a massive electric bill if you don't conserve energy. On the positive side…There are no heating bills.

There is some crime here. The weekly police report in the San Pedro Sun is dominated by arrests for small amounts of cannabis and petty theft. Armed robbery is rare. Thefts are perpetrated by people who cannot find work and have lots of little mouths to feed. Jobs are scarce and theft is not scarce during the slow season.

Our golf cart was stolen and recovered. Our friends who own Ritchie's store also had their cart stolen. They found their cart, and it wasn't in the lagoon where carts sometimes end up after the parts have been sold. SierraSky's new bike was stolen from our yard. She forgot to lock it one night and it was gone by morning. Anything that isn't tied down and locked is stolen, and sometimes the locked items get taken too. Hold onto your possessions if you come here, or be prepared to let go of strong attachments to them.

We have heard that there are billions of mosquitoes here, but they are worse in Wisconsin by a long-shot. We live right on the sea where the breeze keeps them at bay. It is rumored that the south and west sides of the island have a serious mosquito problem. Mosquitoes on Ambergris Caye rarely carry malaria, but there are occasional reports of dengue fever. I have also heard of the parasite problem concerning the Bot Fly in mainland Belize. It's pretty hard to forget the story I heard of a person's experience with a "termite rainfall" when tens of thousands of termites fell from the trees on them when they were hiking in the jungle. To date, I have not had that experience in Belize.

There are lizards, geckos, and iguanas everywhere and they come in every size and shape. The crabs are always underfoot at night as they hunt for their dinner. We expected to see scorpions, exotic spiders, and a variety of snakes, but have not seen a single one. We have talked with locals who have been here fifty years and have never seen one either.

Wait! There's more... If the heat, the electric bill, the crime, and the bugs didn't alarm you, I'll describe a few more things that might not suit your fancy in these parts.

The majority of San Pedranos are hard working and they are still very poor. The leading industry is tourism, and believe me, this is no Cancun. Although begging is illegal there are quite a few kids and adults who wouldn't work a job if it was offered to them. They will accost you and ask outright for money! They are usually strangers, but sometimes even acquaintances become brazen. There are locals who think that Caucasians are made of money. They see you as a walking wallet, and will try to squeeze some money out of you any way they can. We have been approached by people who told us "My husband was murdered last night," "My sister is very ill and needs an operation," " I have run out of my medication and will die without it," "I haven't eaten in seven days" and other tall tales. We help them if at all possible, but try not to give them money. Once you give cash, you have opened a door that is very hard to close...

Everyone has a cousin with a house that we should buy, a store for sale, or a great restaurant that their aunt owns that we should try. It is rather amusing once you get used to it. Coconut Leo attempts to sell me a mint plant, a banana tree, coconut juice, or a coconut picked in our own yard almost every day. The little neighbor boys come on a regular basis to see if I need my sandy lawn raked. My neighbor asks if I need my nails done whenever I see her.

The primary schools here are exceptional. The one and only high school on the island receives students from ten primary schools, is overcrowded, and short on staff. Some graduates go to college in Belize or abroad. Most of the San Pedrano boys enter their family's fishing business or take a job in the tourist industry at a young age. These are jobs that do not require higher education. Many young women begin having children at age sixteen. The high school drop-out rate continues to be addressed by educators looking for a solution to this dilemma.

Our experience has taught us that Belize is the "factory-seconds" capital of the western world! I am now convinced that the stories about the U.S. sending all of its rejected products and factory seconds, to third world countries is a fact. We bought a can opener that you have to operate backwards. Almost every pair of goggles I have purchased are defective. Scissors last two days. The water dispenser rattles, the fan keeps falling apart, the toaster only cooks on one side, and pretty much every toy we buy for SierraSky has been an obvious reject. We don't buy tennis shoes for her in Belize anymore. They fall apart in a few days.

We go to Chetumal, Mexico, where we get quality goods at much cheaper prices. If it's a reject or a "train-wreck special" it's probably stamped, "Rush Order, Ship to Belize!" It is a popular notion that "Murphy's law" originated right here in Belize.

We could go on and on. There are soooooo many things about this Pan-American country that are very different from what we were used to therefore we have "Not All Hummingbirds & Butterflies II.

"A great fortune depends on luck, a small one on diligence." China

Not All Hummingbirds and Butterflies-

Part Two

We have made it abundantly clear by now that we love it here in San Pedro Town. It has a very spiritual vibe. We choose to embrace all of the wonderful things that Belize has to offer and live with the less convenient side of island life. Some people dream of a tropical paradise in their future. For those who may not want to stay in the United States, are seeking a simpler life-style, and are thinking of moving to San Pedro, we must point out a few more challenging realities of living here.

Transportation. Most people walk to their destination. There are many golf carts, taxi's and a few trucks being used but it is the minority of people who own them. In fact, you are not allowed to own a golf cart unless you are a resident. The town and streets were not built or designed for vehicles. This used to be a fishing village that could only be reached by boat. The roads are narrow and only the central part of downtown is brick-paved, the rest is sand, rocks, pot-holes and gravel.

The town is busy with taxis that are often driven too fast. They only allow about 6 inches between you and disaster. It's hard to believe that there aren't more accidents! Vehicles frequently run cyclists off the road and they nearly hit tourists that are standing out in the middle of the street, unaware of the dangerous driving conditions.

We prefer to walk most of the time because the roads are so bumpy and bouncy. There are six inch high speed bumps that make it uncomfortable to travel faster than 5 mph! There are very few sidewalks, except on Front Street and areas with high pedestrian traffic. The golf carts grind the sandy streets into a fine powder and dust everything in their vicinity as they pass by. People who drive too fast leave a cloud of dust in their wake. Often, it is the tourists in rented golf carts who drive around at high speeds and cause near-accidents at every corner. You should plan on doing a lot of walking when you come to Ambergris Caye, or rent a bicycle. Be sure to lock it, wherever you park it, as they seem to mysteriously disappear when not attended to.

The sand is everywhere. When the wind blows, which it does for most of the year, it blows sand into every nook and cranny. I never really understood the "dusting" concept when I lived in the Midwest. Now I have to dust the house daily, and sweep the floors three times a day. We live on the beach and the sand blows right through the screens. Somehow, the sand finds its way into our bed every night. It's like sleeping on the beach. The streets used to be so full of sand that you would sink to your ankles. That is why going barefoot is a tradition on the island. Most people wear flip flops now that the amount of sand in the streets has been greatly reduced.

Dressing up and wearing high heels. You will only see women wearing heels if they work in a bank or office building or if they are going out dancing downtown (where it is paved) at a club like Jaguar's where there is a real floor. Countless restaurants and bars have sand floors. If you are the type who likes to dress up, and wear make-up and heels, save it for the nightlife. The heat and humidity in the afternoon will melt your make-up right off of your face! Many of the local women wear heavy make-up when they go out at night and I am always amazed to see more than a few pairs of stilettos come out after dark. Belizeans love the 1980's and they embrace the Eighties "look" and music. Big hair, beaucoup make-up, flashy earrings, six-inch heels, busty cleavage and short, short dresses. "Punta" dancing is part of the night time culture in Belize and is here to stay. It is sexy, erotic and extremely explicit! When you first see Punta dancing it may shock you. Eventually you become accustomed to it and may even be tempted to join in.

No drive-through food chains. If you like McDonalds and Burger King, you are out-of-luck down here. There are no franchises allowed in Belize, and this has really helped to keep the "mom & pop" restaurants alive. There are plenty of tiny food stands, small deli's and little restaurants that serve inexpensive dishes that are worth waiting for.

I will never forget the day I asked my landlord which day was garbage pick-up day? She said, "Everyday." I couldn't believe it! The trash is picked up six days a week, even the garbage men get Sundays off. Garbage disposal is tricky. There is minimal recycling on the island. It is limited to coke and beer bottles. It was very hard for us to get used to this at first. We had been trained in the U.S. to recycle everything. When we arrived in Belize we washed and saved every plastic and glass container that we came home with. After it began to pile up, we started giving it away to neighbors and friends. We finally started throwing some things away. Disposing of recyclables felt wrong after being conditioned to sort them. We try to keep our carbon footprint to a bare minimum.

Recently, a waste/generation/composition study has been carried out to determine the type of waste that is generated on the island. All waste is collected and transported by barges to the Regional Sanitary Landfill located in Mile 24 on the Western Highway.

"No tickee, no washee!" Most San Pedranos hand-wash their laundry and hang it out to dry. There is only one laundromat in San Pedro and it is expensive. You can drop off your laundry at certain homes, where the woman of the house will clean, dry, and fold your clothes for a price. Not very many people own their own laundry machines. Water and electricity are expensive. Our water bill is double what we paid in the States. Many San Pedranos still collect rain water in cisterns, and use it for dishes, showers, toothbrushing, laundry, etc. If you do hang your clothes out in your yard, you have to be sure to bring them in as soon as they are dry. This prevents them from being coated from the sand and sea salt in the air. They can also be baked hard and dry from the intense sunshine. Getting it just-right is a fine art.

We don't have the vast selection of products here that we enjoyed in the States! Most goods are available at one store or another, but occasionally there will be a product that you really want, and cannot find on the island. Items like "Tom's" toothpaste or "Avalon" shampoo or "Classico" tomato sauce and pro-biotic supplements do not exist here. I have had to settle for "Crest" toothpaste, "Tres-Semme" conditioner, and (I never-thought-it-would-come-to-this) "Ragu" spaghetti sauce. There is no matzo ball mix, horseradish, or good sausage on the island. We ask our friends to bring specialty goods to us when they come for a visit. My sister in law was very sweet, and mailed me my favorite shampoo and toothpaste but I had to pay 60% duty on it. I hate to be picky, but sometimes a person likes what they like.

The doctors and medical services here in Belize, are the best in Central America. Belize actually has free healthcare. If you go to the Poly Clinic II, you can see a doctor for free, but they expect a donation of whatever amount you can spare. If you need surgery the doctors at the clinic will refer you to a specialist or a surgeon. Generally, it costs much less than the same operation would in the States. A cat-scan, with diagnostics, costs $225USD. An Echo-gram $125. A root-canal, with a crown $100. An ultra-sound, $30. Most hospitals use the latest technological advances that are available in America and Europe. There are nine doctors on the island, and they are top-notch general practitioners. They do charge a small fee for their services.

What about emergencies? Unfortunately, there is not a "Flight for Life" helicopter anymore, the island can't afford it. If an emergency health crisis occurs that requires immediate hospitalization, you may be out of luck. There isn't a hospital in San Pedro. There are local physicians that list their 24-hour phone number, and will see you in the middle of the night if you can reach them! In the event of a severe health matter, you have to book a flight to Belize City or Chetumal, Mexico during regular business hours. . . It it is my understanding that the doctors will not operate without cash on the spot so it is a good idea to keep a few thousand dollars on hand, just in case.

Don't forget the hurricanes. This was the 2nd busiest tropical storm season in history with nineteen named storms, ten of which were hurricanes. There is a constant vigil six months of the year, as we watch and wonder if each hurricane will come to our shores. When it does everything gets flooded, trees blow over, wires come down, tourists are flown out in a mandatory evacuation, and the damaged infra-structure can be down for long periods of time.

) We are in the minority here. There are a few thousand ex-patriots from the U.S. and Canada that live here in San Pedro. If you are Caucasian, you are part of the minority here. Some people are very uncomfortable being surrounded by peoples whose skin colors range from "cream in your coffee" to "so black they are purple!" We think that the people of Belize are beautiful in every color and size. Attitude is everything. Many types of ethnicities and heritages, whether it be Mestizo, Kriol, Garifuna, Mayan, or a mix of all of the above live together here happily and peacefully. If you can't feel comfortable being in the minority, San Pedro is not for you.

No Work/No Employment. There aren't enough jobs for all of the people. You have to create your own work to generate an income. You must have an idea and a skill, trade or talent, and be willing to work very hard for very little money. Most gringos that reside here have a steady income from abroad. This is a good plan...

Got Sharks? The Bull Shark is a shark common worldwide in warm, shallow waters along coasts. The bull shark is well known for its unpredictable, often aggressive behavior. Since bull sharks frequently dwell in shallow waters, they may be more dangerous to humans than any other species of shark. Along with tiger sharks and great white sharks they are among the three shark species most likely to attack humans. They have been spotted inside our reef on many occasions. They wander in to feed at night and can be 7 to 14 feet long! There have not been any reported attacks off the shores of the Island of Ambergris Caye as of today. We do NOT swim after dark as a precaution.

We tolerate those pesky sand flies also known as "sand-fleas" and "no-see-ums." They are so small that it makes it very hard to detect them as they relentlessly attack you. The next morning when you see the bright red bites on your ankles and legs, you realize how many times you were bitten. The bites really itch and are considered more irritating than a mosquitoes bite. They mostly attack at dusk and dawn. They nest in underground burrows below the sand and their nests can contain millions of the tiny parasites. Bug repellant can deter them. They are not a constant nuisance in our life. They are only around if it has rained recently, or if you are near a body of brackish water. They aren't usually active during the day and at night.

The Unspeakable: COCK-ROACHES! (la cucaracha) My mom warned me that there are huge cock-roaches in the tropics. I can hear her saying "Eewwwwwwww! They are so HIDEOUS!" Sure enough. You have to keep your house SUPER, DUPER clean of all food scraps, sugar, and any crumbs or garbage. We take our garbage out after every meal. We don't have any roaches in our house due to our diligence, but, we have seen them and mom was right, HIDEOUS! EWWWWWWW! It's something about the way they scurry! Some of the islanders use the big ones for fish bait.

Occasional power and water outages. From time to time they have to turn off the power to fix the lines, clean the generators, and continue to improve and expand the infrastructure. The whole island will experience a planned black-out. It is so dark when it happens at night that you feel like you can reach out and touch the stars! We never know how long it will take until the power comes back on, but the black-outs can last from two minutes to a whole day.

Over the Easter holiday last year, there was an unusual amount of tourists and approximately 8,000 Belizean family members who came over from the mainland to celebrate the five day week-end. Unfortunately, the water pressure was insufficient for that many extra guests on the island. Only a trickle came out of our pipes for several days. I sure hope they have improved on the water system's capacity by next year when they return like clockwork.

Crocodiles! Let's not forget the minor crocodile problem that we have on the island. Yes, a few dogs have gone missing. There was a crocodile sanctuary in southern Belize that would accept problem "crocs", but it was burned-down by members of the village who were afraid that the crocodiles were eating children. Now the crocodile rescue team, A.C.E.S., has moved to the island and removes problem crocodiles. When they are released in a far away location, they often return to their old haunts here on the island. Even the crocodiles love it here. Once you have been to San Pedro Town, it is hard to stay away.

Something to make you sit and ponder. The city sewer and septic systems are fragile here, so all of the used waste-paper goes into a garbage can next to the toilet . . . . . yes, all of it! The soiled paper is taken out regularly in our house, but some places are not so prompt about it. It can be especially distressing when you visit the bathroom in many restaurants, bars, or your hotel lobby.

If you are interested in moving to San Pedro and this information hasn't deterred you, a realistic evaluation about Belize MUST come from a visit (or two)! Any ideas you may entertain about the island's primitive ways, numerous shortcomings, and lack of modern conveniences, will seem to disappear rather quickly once you have arrived. It reminds us of the "Old West" and we are the cowboys. It's not for everyone. It's for the risk-takers, with pioneering spirits, who love a challenge and don't mind a little heat.

"Adversity produces human ability, not necessarily wealth."

Chinese proverb

Appendix II

THE HUSBAND'S CHAPTER

Shall we begin with a cold one, gentlemen?

(This chapter is entitled "The Husband's Chapter" for two reasons: 1. It was written by my husband and 2. For those of you who have a husband who won't take the time to read a long wordy book, they can read this chapter and get most of the information covered in the book, with plenty of statistics and humor.)

Buenos dias amigos y amigas! I would like to share some of my casual observations, in no particular order, about Belize. We hope you have enjoyed our journey of moving to the tropics so far, and that you find this list interesting, informative, and occasionally amusing. There is still a whole lot to learn for us "gringos in Belize."

Jerry Jeff Walker says "Belize is weird, man! Everything they do around here is done differently than anywhere else. It'll make you wonder a bit if you've just arrived here for the first time. So, just go along with the way they do things in San Pedro and you'll enjoy every minute of your visit to paradise."

When Jerry Jeff was visiting here recently, he told us a true story about meeting Dr. Rosita Arvigo, the author of "Rainforest Remedies," on a flight home to Texas. They struck up a conversation on the plane and he was telling her about his various maladies. She said she would be happy to send him some herbs from Belize to be used for making various teas and poultices that might be helpful to him. Sure enough, two weeks later, the package arrived from Rosita. Inside the box he found 3 sprigs of herbs and a hefty rock. He was puzzled. So he called her up and told her "Much obliged, Rosita. I got the package today, and I remember our little talk about the plants and how to use them. But for the life of me, I can't remember what that rock was for." She laughed, and began to explain that "In Belize they won't ship packages under a certain weight, so I had to put a rock in the box for ballast! I hope the herbs help with your problem."

Jerry Jeff laughed and said to us, "See what I mean? Belize is Weeeeird, man!" . . . And we agree with him. Now...on to some of the typical island stuff that we have gathered to date:

Two things go through your fingers like water in Belize. They are water, and Belizean money.

The U.S. dollar is worth two Belizean dollars. My dollar is worth twice as much, but it only buys half as much. EVERYTHING costs more on an island.

Hence the saying, "Ambergris Caye; to make a million dollars, bring two million!"

There are no less than 100 grocery stores scattered in an area of two square miles. There are five super-markets, and the other 95 are little 'Ma & Pa' stores in the front room of people's homes. They all seem to be doing well.

We don't do one-stop shopping here. You buy paper goods at one store, meat at another, canned goods at the smaller shops, fruits and vegetables at various stands. On 'shopping day' we often visit 7 locations.

Zoning is still getting established here. Next to a house you have a shop, and next to that a cantina, and then another house, and another bar, etc. You can open a restaurant in your home, and open and close as you please. Liquor licenses can be readily obtained if you file and pay. Ice cold beer is sold everywhere, like water. Belikin beer is considered to be its own food-group in Belize.

Music is played LOUD here. From early morning, until late at night. It goes way back to the man who had the first radio on the island. He blasted it at full volume in order to share his music with anyone within earshot. An island tradition was born. It lives on today, at high volume. I dare you to try and sleep... Music is extremely loud at the clubs. You have to shout to hear yourself and the music reverberates through your body. Belizeans won't dance unless the music is deafening. Some bars are open until 5am. Then the breakfast cantinas open. Then back to the bars ☺

The island is a tourist destination. The use of alcohol at any time of day is not only acceptable, it is encouraged. The more tourists drink, the more they spend! Many ex-patriots have succumbed to the charms of good quality Caribbean rum at $6.00 per litre, and at 6:00 am!

Rum Punch is the island drink. It can be found anywhere. Stewed chicken with rice and red beans is the national dish. It can also be found everywhere. They are both considered to be "comfort foods".

There are over 136 ways to prepare chicken in Belize. And they are ALL delicious! Bar-B-Que chicken cooked over natural charcoal is available on every corner. It is the #1 way that Belizeans enjoy chicken, and plenty of diverse recipes abound. The competition for the best BBQ sauce is constantly being played out with new and tastier recipes. On Saturdays, you can choose from a dry-rub, jerk, sweet sauce, garlic-onion, malt vinegar, sprite-sauce, plain-char, smoked, ginger & lime, curry and black-pepper. The list of recipes is endless, and very tasty. Come down here just for the chicken Bar-B-Que. It's fantastic!

Fish are plentiful. Lydia caught six snappers yesterday in an hour! Snapper fillets sell for $5USD per pound at the fish and lobster dock down at the lagoon. They are caught and sold every morning. They are so fresh and delicious that you can enjoy them for breakfast.

Lobster is a way of life here. Hundreds of thousands of pounds are exported from Belize each year. Most of the local restaurants serve a lobster 'specialty' and you will never get tired of trying a new way to taste fresh lobster. Lobster Fest is around June 29th. Most fisherman bring back 100 lbs or more on opening day. Prices can go as low as $18 BZD per pound. ($9.00 USD) Lobster season begins on June 15th. When lobster fest begins, they immediately start cooking it in Central Park for the next 24 hours. You can order it broiled with garlic butter, but Belizeans consider this a waste of good lobster meat. With all of the spicy combinations available to us, it is a lobster lover's dream come true. So much lobster...so little time!

The arts of air-conditioning, refrigeration, and ice making have been perfected here. They make our Wisconsin cooling systems seem 'third-world'. They have digital temperature gauges on their beer coolers so it is easy to choose your favorite place for a 'cold one'. The average temp for a beer is 17* Fahrenheit. Beer freezes at 16 degrees.

Belize is originally Mayan country. Currently, Mestizos, Spanish, Kriol, Garifunas, East Indians and Chinese make up the majority. There are numerous Guatemalans, Hondurans, Nicaraguans and lots of Lebanese. There is a strong Rastafarian population and some Cuban restauranteurs. There is a large Mennonite group, which includes farmers, shipbuilders and furniture makers, and there are numerous Mexican immigrants. This mix of cultures raises the bar on local cuisine and makes the food an unbelievable experience that must be seen and tasted to appreciate.

There are ten schools on the island. All of them have higher standards than the average school in the United States. Kindergarten (Infant 1) is actually 1st grade. They teach mathematics, spelling, reading, writing, social studies, language arts, general science, health science, problem solving, along with computer skills and comprehension. Back in Wisconsin they are being taught the 'ABC's at this same age.

Belizean women are prepared for childbirth and childcare by the age of 15. By this age they have been taught many skills including, housekeeping, homemaking, cooking, sewing and making clothing. They also prepare foods to sell on the street to help the family's income. These skills are highly valued and the mother is the core of the Belizean family. She is held in very high esteem and respected by this culture. No mother is ever neglected. This is a matter of pride and they will happily care for older women until their last day on this earth. There are very few old-folks-homes here.

It is not un-common to see a forty-eight year old great-grandmother walking with her thirty-two year old daughter, accompanied by her sixteen year old daughter, carrying her own new-born baby. Four generations in less than fifty years.

Mosquitoes are more un-manageable in Wisconsin than here on the "mosquito coast."

The most common foods are stewed chicken with beans and rice, corn flour tortillas, stew beans, salbutes, garnaches, papusas, salsas, fresh ceviche, (shrimp, conch, or lobster) ground steak, pork chops, steaks, ham, sausages, and fish of every variety. A taco or burrito can be made from almost anything in the imagination. Fruits and vegetables are a big part of every meal served. Several types of cabbage coleslaw and potato salads are popular as side dishes. Turkey is expensive and considered a delicacy! With all the fabulous vegetables that are locally grown...asparagus is found only in cans eleven months of the year. You can purchase fresh asparagus in July for $10 per pound. It's the same with jalapeno peppers. (too hot to grow them.) It is the habanero pepper that is king around here!

It is possible to purchase almost any American food item you desire on the island. Until fifteen years ago the island had never seen pizza, burgers, hot dogs, or french-fries. Fish, rice, and beans were the staple foods until the gringos arrived.

Madonna wrote a song called "Isla Bonita" about her visits here. It truly is a beautiful island.

The kids wear uniforms to school every day. On Fridays, (rag-day) if you pay one dollar, the kids can wear whatever they please and the money goes to charity.

People walk down the street smiling in Belize. Happy and

approachable, they are always willing to talk for a bit and help you whenever they can. In Belize they say "just ask!" It is refreshing to see such happy faces, every day.

Chains and franchises do not exist in this country. If you must have McDonald's, Burger King, Home Depot, Wal-Mart, Pizza Hut, or KFC, you simply take a boat-ride (water-taxi, 90 minutes) to Chetumal, Mexico to get your fix. Belize will NEVER cave in to big business.

This island was a coconut plantation in the 19th century. We recently harvested 50 coconuts from one of the 4 coconut trees in our front yard. There are another 150 growing on the same tree in different stages of maturity. If you do not harvest them when they are ripe and ready, a 15 lb coconut can fall on your head from 40 ft high and cause a deadly accident. Don't fall asleep under a coconut tree!

It takes one year to mature a coconut. At this point they will provide you with coconut water, coconut milk, coconut jelly, and coconut meat that is sweet and nutritious. Coconut oil is very good for you, as recent research will confirm. The liquid inside young coconuts can be used as a substitute for blood plasma.

There are twelve different varieties of coconuts on this island. All distinctly delicious. Cooking with coconut milk is very common. It is used in soups, fish dishes, and rice. Many popular tropical drinks require coconut products in one form or another. Coconut water is sold everywhere and is prized at Belizean weddings to make a gin, mint and coconut juice drink called "coco-loco." You must try the coconut rums.

Limes are a staple food here. Limes are abundant and come in every size and shape. They are used for lime juice, (local lemonade) eating, cooking, drinking, cleaning, and several hangover recipes. You can usually buy them, eight for a dollar.

If you want a lemon in Belize, bring it on the plane with you. I haven't seen one since we've been here.

Because of the abundance of these two items...we put "de lime in de coconut, and drink it all up"! (Harry Nilsson) It does relieve de belly ache. And don't forget to enjoy lime and coconut cheesecake...mmmmm...mmmm!

Walking is the main means of transportation here. There is no hurry and the sandy terrain is always pleasant on bare feet. Bicycles are very popular. Mothers ride with their children on the handlebars, or on the crossbar, or in a basket. It is not uncommon to see three kids on a bike with their mom.

Golf carts are becoming more and more popular for transportation. The island has no air pollution thanks to the sea breezes that blow it all away. Gas-powered carts are on all the cobblestone streets, and are definitely here to stay. Thankfully, for the safety of everyone, they only go ten miles per hour. We cannot imagine getting into a car that does 75 mph again. It seems ridiculously fast and unsafe now that we are living here, on "island time."

If you love to fish, but don't love to cook 'em... take the big fish you caught to ANY restaurant on the island, and for a small fee ($5 USD) they will happily cook it and serve it to you with all the trimmings. ONLY in Belize.

Meats, fish and other foods are cooked in banana leaves. It is the old way of cooking, and it brings something wonderful to the flavor of fresh foods. Bananas here are tree-ripened, very sweet, and come in four varieties. Plantains are sold everywhere, and are used in soups and stews. Both bananas and plantains are delicious, when fried.

Belize is one of 56 countries that speak English as their official language. Beyond the obvious ones, Australia, New Zealand, England, Ireland, Scotland, Canada, and the United States, there are 21 English speaking countries and non-sovereign entities in the Caribbean, and 18 in Africa.

Some of the world's freshest air, rich in oxygen from surrounding jungles and plant-life, blows through here every day of the year. The "trade winds" come all the way from Africa, with no industrial pollution in its path. It is a very pleasant experience to breathe clean fresh air all the time. It makes you feel energized! Serious lung problems are uncommon in this area of the world.

Because of the relatively small population of Belize, there is limited demand for large production food stuff. Items such as chickens, eggs, fruits, and vegetables are produced on small farms in the Mennonite community, and in much smaller batches than in the U.S. or Mexico. Because of the lowered demand and smaller production, the chickens, beef, lamb and pork are "free-range" and no growth hormones or "egg-on" stimulants are used. It would not be cost-effective for the growers. The fruits and vegetables are treated with a minimum of pesticides or herbicides for the same reason. We appreciate the fact that these additives to our delicious foods are just too expensive for the local farmers to use. Small country, small demand, everybody wins.

The Poly-Clinic II is a medical center on Ambergris Caye sponsored by the Belizean government. Treatment for every type of illness is free. They ask for a donation of $5. We have had some very positive experiences at this clinic, including a full dental exam in a clean, all modern dentist office with new high-tech equipment. This led to a root canal (painless) and crown for SierraSky costing only $100. (U.S. price would've been around

$2500!) They treat all patients without ANY insurance or moneys.

There is a very modern hospital in Belize City. It is only twenty minutes away by plane. Serious and life threatening problems are treated there. No insurance card is required to enter the hospital. Reasonably priced services are paid for in cash. This reduces the overall costs of medical care.

Every kid on the island has swim-fins and a spear-gun. It is the quickest, sure-fire method of attaining a meal. Mom say's "Go get some lunch or dinner" and the fish is on the table in thirty minutes. Why wait for a fish to bite…when you can spear them? They learn to use a spear-gun at a very young age, and I have never heard of an accident; only about the wonderful meals they caught so quickly, and efficiently.

There is no "FAST" speed in Belize. Don't bother trying to prompt or hurry anyone here, for any reason. You will receive a quizzical look. One of the favorite responses of the island servers when you request faster service is, "Right now, Right now!" Which translated from Creole means: "your big hurry just added another 45 minutes to your lunch-hour, gringo"! Standing in line is a part of life here, and a big part of social networking. The longer the line…the longer the chat. They seek the longer line here. "What's the hurry? We follow 'island time' around here" is a typical response to the gringo's need to rush everything along. If you want to eat lunch promptly at noon…order it at breakfast time.

Although Belize is sub-tropical, people come down here in the summertime from, Texas, Arizona, New Mexico, Louisiana, Florida, and even South Carolina just to cool off. We have made friends with local shopkeepers who live in Miami. They spend their summers here because it is so hot and humid in Florida. The Caribbean Sea is around 84 degrees year-round. The trade winds blow across the water and cool the island to 84 degrees. Its nature's air conditioner. It can be 110 degrees in Belize City just forty miles away, and be 84 degrees here. The temperature rarely varies more than seven degrees between daytime and evenings.

The "rainy season" is from June 1st until November 30th. The rain must fall at a rate of 1" every 5 days to qualify as the rainy season. We had a record 10 inches on May 19th, 6" more on June 26th, another 4" deluge on July 18th, and on August 10th we had 5 inches. In September it has rained three times around 2" each time. It does not rain every day. And when it does rain, the sun re-appears within a few hours. We expected it to rain every day and that is NOT how it is down here.

The people of Belize are a mix of many ethnicities. There are native people here who are very white with green eyes, red hair and freckles. They are descended from Irish and English sailors. Every shade of skin-tone is represented by the locals. We see many tall and slender men and women descended from African tribes (escaped slaves) with almond shaped eyes (Chinese), and high cheekbones (Mayan), with sleek noses (East Indian), and they all have beautiful white teeth and smiles to match. The people of Belize would win a world-wide beauty pageant, hands down. Even the Tahitian women would be envious of the typical beauties on this island. No one here can point a finger at someone else. Everybody is racially mixed and proud of it. It's a good leveler.

The largest export here (after lobster meat) is sugar products including rum. We are in the sugar capital of the Caribbean. There are cane fields all over the mainland, and raw, stripped sugar cane stalks are sold to children in the open markets to chew on. Raw cane juice is delicious and has many health benefits. Sugar is dirt-cheap and comes in many grades of refinement and colors. Candy is big business, and so are sweetbreads and cakes of all kinds. There are 3 bakeries within a mile of us, and they all stay busy. Yes, there is a "Sugar-fest." Quality dental care is available to everyone.

We are fortunate to be in the center of the Cocoa Bean growers, traders, and processors. Swiss and Belgium buyers show up every year to purchase the best beans in enormous quantities. The annual "Cocoa Bean Festival" sells organic home-made chocolates in every size, shape and flavor imaginable! With all the different flavors of chocolate around, you may think you died and went to heaven! Dark chocolate can be as high as 87% pure cocoa. Chocolate is a food group in Belize, and they take it very seriously here on the island. Is your mouth watering yet?

Swimming is the national past-time here. The Caribbean Sea is clean, warm, salty, and it makes you very buoyant. The children are always busy in the water playing, laughing, and squealing joyfully! People swim in their clothes here. If they are hot, and the water is nearby, they just jump in. Belizeans over forty don't swim as often as the kids. After swimming every day of their lives since early childhood, they prefer to leave it to the young. No-one swims at night. Nocturnal feeders from beyond the reef come into the shallows after dark to look for food. Why tempt fate?

Crime has never really been a problem here. Everyone knows everyone else, and they all come from large extended families. It is an embarrassment to be reported as a criminal in the local papers, and it brings shame upon your family's good name. This is a powerful deterrent. People don't commit crimes, because everybody will know it if you do. It's an island, and there is nowhere to hide from prosecution. Criminal behavior is socially un-acceptable in Belize.

Five years ago the crime-rate on Ambergris Caye was 2.02%, but there has been an economic crash here too. It caused a slowing down of the tourist industry, and fewer hotel projects being built. In 2008, most Belizeans had steady work, and plenty of money to provide for their families. Today, many locals are looking for work. They say "desperate people do desperate things." Men come from the mainland looking for work, and end up stealing just to feed their families. Theft is the main crime committed here. The crime rate is up by 7% and the islanders are outraged! They are determined to stop crime and restore "La Isla Bonita" to its former crime-free state. Violent crime is extremely rare. This is one of the safest communities in the world to raise a child. We never worry about the "tremendous increase in crime" in the headlines, on our peaceful island.

We have been here for 33 months. Gasoline has gone DOWN in price by $1 per gallon. (golf carts get around 50 mpg) Propane for cooking has decreased by $9 per tank. Can you imagine energy costs going backwards in the States?

Recently, we have had five "near-misses". Hurricane Alex (in late June) hit the coast 30 miles from here. We had some 50 mph gusts and an inch of rain. Hurricane Karl (late August) came directly through here as a tropical storm. A little bit of rain and wind. No damages. Tropical storm Matthew visited briefly. It brought terrible floods and mudslides for our neighboring countries. Paula brushed by us, and hurricane Richard went straight to Belize City with extensive damage reported there. We got some waves and a rain shower. The islanders say Belize has always been "blessed". The last BIG hurricane was Hattie in 1961. It tore up the mainland but spared the island. We keep a radar vigil, just the same…

Common-law marriage is recognized in many countries, including the U.S. This usually involves filing a short form at the local courthouse after seven years of co-habitation. It is all very legal. Here in Belize common-law marriage is recognized after proof of ONE NIGHT together. (This information comes straight from the Dept. of Immigration and Naturalization.) This is how they deal with the numerous pregnancies and problems that arrive at the

Magistrates' desk when people live together and have property and children they are fighting over. One result of this law is that Belizean boyfriends ALWAYS get home by sunrise. You will see them walking the streets in a mass exodus just before the break of dawn. Not quite ready for a wife, I suppose... One-night-stands take on a different meaning around here. Don't get drunk and pass out, you'll wake up hitched!

The water here is de-salinated by a modern water plant and is potable. The children drink it growing up with no ill effects. We use it for showering, dishes, tooth-brushing, etc. We choose to purchase our drinking/cooking water from a local company (Crystal) that uses fresh water and a reverse osmosis purification system. It is clean tasting and cheap. Five gallons of "filtered" water in the States costs between $5.50 and $9 per bottle. Here we pay $1.75 USD for a much better product and you can buy it everywhere. It is also delivered to your door, free of charge.

The island has a definite "rhythm". There is a time to eat, a time to rest, and a time to play. The island people are aware of this and participate in these special rhythms. They all seem to leave their homes for work at the same time each morning. The lunch hour brings everyone out to the street vendors serving their daily specials. In the evening everybody walks in the cool breezes during the gorgeous sunset. The Belizean women walk with a gentle sway in their hips that mimics the coconut trees moving in the warm breezes. It is remarkable to see the timing of all this.

"Political correctness" does not exist in Belize. You can enter a bar with a drink or bring your own food into a restaurant. You can walk out of a bar with a drink and enjoy it on any public street without offending anyone. When purchasing an icy-cold beer in a store you can open it and drink it right there! Strolling around with an open drink is commonplace. It is illegal to drink and drive. It is not illegal to be intoxicated.

Smoking grass is illegal in Belize. There are strict penalties enforced for breaking the drug laws. If you choose to break the law and are caught, you will be arrested and meet with the local magistrate and a fine will be levied. Best to keep it cool, man...

Cigarette smoking is accepted here. Most restaurants and bars are open-air and very few establishments enforce a non-smoking policy. Huge Cuban cigars are smoked everywhere you go and the breezes blow the smoke away instantly. It is rare to hear a smoking complaint.

There is no enforcement of laws regarding public urination. When you gotta' go, you gotta' go and restrooms are few and far between. It is considered impolite to face the public when relieving yourself. When you walk along the beach at night you will see men (and women) standing behind palm trees taking care of business. Gentlemen, please be discreet.

When you are passing by in your cart and you say "Hi" to someone, the response is often "Bye." The first few times this happened we wondered, "What? Do they want to make sure we keep moving on? What did I ever do to them? After a few more "Bye" responses to our "Hi" we figured it out. If it is nighttime, they say "good night" just like you would say "good morning."

Bowen & Bowen is the only brewery in Belize. They make a strong, tasty beer in the English tradition called Belikin Lager. (Sorry...we don't have enough to export.) It's very dry, hoppy, full bodied and delicious with a clean finish. "Belikin Stout" is the local favorite and is 6.5 % alcohol by volume. Best bang for your buck! They also brew "Lighthouse Lager," (less alcohol and calories) and "Guiness Stout" (7.5%) by international license. Around Christmas they brew an herbal seasonal beer called "Sorrel Stout" and another during the summer months called "Verona." Heineken is imported from Holland and Red-Stripe is imported from Jamaica. We don't complain about the limited selection. Seven well crafted beers are better than 100 inferior selections!

You now have all the information you will need to come to Belize and have a fabulous time. Look me up when you get here...I'll buy your first icy-cold Belikin lager!

"Passionate kiss like spider's web, soon lead to undoing of fly."

Acknowledgements

We would like to offer our sincere thanks to our friends and family members who gave us their constant encouragement and support during the creation of this book. It was their contagious enthusiasm that made it possible for us to reach the finish line. We wish all of you continued good health and great prosperity.

SierraSky, Cindi-bear and Jo-mama, Rose and Max Estes, Frank, Joy and Winston, Suzanne Helene Roe, Richard Cleland and Aunt Janet, Diane Quicksilver, Fred Seegers, Miss Tina Lendman, Terry Tang, Miss Maria from Pelican Internet, and The Ancient Asian Sages

We would like to offer a special thanks to Jerry Jeff and Susan Walker who inspired us by leading the way to paradise.

We would like to thank our Belizean and ex-patriot friends in Ambergris Caye for their patience and understanding of our gringo ways. Thank you for your support, encouragement, help and guidance on our journey!

Mr. Frank Panton, Miss Joy Flowers, and Winston, Mike Kuhn of Tropic Air, Ched and Staff of Reef Adventures, Miss Sherry Moore, Miss Shelly from Ecologic Divers, Mr. Dick Gentry, Mr. Enrique Staines and Family, Miss Monica, Dale Wallace from Wallace Custom Guitars, Oscar from My Secret Deli, Robert Cunningham and Berta-Lydia, Jo Castleberry and the Ladies Card Group, Carlo Segura and Family, the Staff of Blue Tang Inn, Tim and Jenny Johnson, Cherylene and Criselda from the Squirrels Nest, Pirate, Robbie of Chuck and Robbie's, Silver, Mein, Wally's Electrical Supply and Family Miss Melanie Paz, Gary Kroeker, Dennisito Wolfe, Wayo and Staff from Wayo's Internet Beach Bar, Miss Anna and Jim, Mash and Family, Dave and Miss Renae,

Miss Wendy Simmons of MOSCOT Vintage Eye Wear, Captain Martin Leslie and Family, Captain Mercedes of the Glass Bottom Boat Tours, Ernie, Miss Karen and Staff from Captain Morgan's Retreat, Miss Charlene, Ernie and Ebby of BC's Beach Bar, Gordon and Lorna, Bill and Connie, Romeo and Staff from Banana Beach, Dulce Wolfe, Dennis Wolfe and the Usual Suspects, Drummer David, Dr. Lerida Rodriguez, Coconut Leo, Cookie from Dready's Bar, Shay Zerfas and Jean Hallet, Tamara and Staff of San Pedro Sun, Ritchie's Supermarket and Family, Miss Addie Martinez and Family, Mr. Kevin Oberholtzer, Daniel and Elodia, Miss Emma, Steve of Pirate's Pizza, Miss Elizabeth, Walter from Pedro's Pizza, Mr. Albert the Wood Carver and Family, Pamela the Cookie Lady, Emilio and Kirsten from Ak' Bol, Simon from TMM Charters and Elena, Katia and Staff from Pampered Paws, Phil and Marie of Gecko Graphics, Bruce "The Breeze" Pickering, Jeff and Michelle and the Staff of Ambergris Brew Company, Kayleen and Garrick from Wet Willy's, Scott from the Palapa Bar, Brandi and Tull, Gino, Miss Char from Art of Touch Massage, Miss Flor Nunez from British Caribbean Bank, the Staff of Caye International Bank, Teacher Carol, Mr. Tino Gonzales and Famiy, Mark and Judy, Dr. Floyd Jackson, Rebecca and Staff at Tackle Box, Captain Antonio Gonzales and Family, Miss Marie and Buddy, Mary and Mark, Charlie and Willie, Judith and R.B., Dan and Theresa of Lagniappe Provisioning, Fritz from Crazy Canuck's Beach Bar, The Lyrical King from the beach, The Greenhouse, David the Dog Whisperer, Kimberly, Hayden and Captain Timo, Diona and Staff from Mojito Bar, Ellis and Omar, SuperBuy Stores, Drummer Dan and Derrick, Polo, Mr. Charlie and Family from Estelle's, The Postmaster and his efficient Staff, Manelly's Ice Cream, Mr. Jex, Miss Celi Jean, Hands, Lori Purdy, John Brandley, Jeff and Pam of Reef Village, Rompe Raja Band, Mandingo from the Lazy Lizard Lounge, and Tino and Miss Stephanie from our favorite BBQ Chicken Stand!

Lydia A. Estes and Robert Kyle Ashton III

Made in the USA
Lexington, KY
04 August 2013